PSYCHOLOGY PRACTITIONER GUIDEBOOKS

EDITORS

Arnold P. Goldstein, Syracuse University
Leonard Krasner, Stanford University & SUNY at Stony Brook
Sol L. Garfield, Washington University in St. Louis

THE PRACTICE OF BRIEF PSYCHOTHERAPY

Pergamon Titles of Related Interest

Beutler ECLECTIC PSYCHOTHERAPY: A Systematic Approach
Brenner THE EFFECTIVE PSYCHOTHERAPIST: Conclusions from
  Practice and Research
Hersen/Kazdin/Bellack THE CLINICAL PSYCHOLOGY HANDBOOK
Higginbotham/West/Forsyth PSYCHOTHERAPY AND BEHAVIOR
  CHANGE: Social, Cultural, and Methodological Perspectives
Kanfer/Goldstein HELPING PEOPLE CHANGE: A Textbook of
  Methods, Third Edition
Kazdin CHILD PSYCHOTHERAPY: Developing and Identifying
  Effective Treatments

Related Journal
(Free sample copies available upon request)

CLINICAL PSYCHOLOGY REVIEW

THE PRACTICE OF BRIEF PSYCHOTHERAPY

SOL L. GARFIELD
Washington University in St. Louis

PERGAMON PRESS
New York • Oxford • Beijing • Frankfurt
São Paulo • Sydney • Tokyo • Toronto

Pergamon Press Offices:

U.S.A.	Pergamon Press, Inc., Maxwell House, Fairview Park, Elmsford, New York 10523, U.S.A.
U.K.	Pergamon Press plc, Headington Hill Hall, Oxford OX3 0BW, England
PEOPLE'S REPUBLIC OF CHINA	Pergamon Press, Qianmen Hotel, Beijing, People's Republic of China
FEDERAL REPUBLIC OF GERMANY	Pergamon Press GmbH, Hammerweg 6, D-6242 Kronberg, Federal Republic of Germany
BRAZIL	Pergamon Editora Ltda, Rua Eça de Queiros, 346, CEP 04011, São Paulo, Brazil
AUSTRALIA	Pergamon Press Australia Pty Ltd., P.O. Box 544, Potts Point, NSW 2011, Australia
JAPAN	Pergamon Press, 8th Floor, Matsuoka Central Building, 1-7-1 Nishishinjuku, Shinjuku-ku, Tokyo 160, Japan
CANADA	Pergamon Press Canada Ltd., Suite 271, 253 College Street, Toronto, Ontario M5T 1R5, Canada

---

Copyright © 1989 Pergamon Press, Inc.

Library of Congress Cataloging in Publication Data

Garfield, Sol L. (Sol Louis), 1918-
 The practice of brief psychotherapy / Sol L. Garfield.
  p. cm. -- (Psychology practitioner guidebooks)
 Bibliography: p.
 Includes index.
 ISBN 0-08-035890-X : ISBN 0-08-035889-6 (pbk.)
 1. Psychotherapy, Brief. I. Title. II. Series.
RC480.55.G37 1989
616.89'14--dc19   88-39392
                                                                      CIP

Printed in the United States of America

∞™ The paper used in this publication meets the minimum requirements of
     American National Standard for Information Sciences -- Permanence of
     Paper for Printed Library Materials, ANSI Z39.48-1984

Contents

Preface

Early in my own career, I became interested in brief psychotherapy, for several reasons. Most of the clients or patients that I saw did not appear interested in long-term therapy of the uncovering kind, many of them showed positive change in 20 sessions or less, and brief therapy clearly was a more efficient form of psychotherapy. Thus, brief psychotherapy was more capable potentially of meeting our society's need for mental health services than were the more traditional long-term therapies.

This view, however, was not shared by a large number of the individuals engaged in psychotherapy in the late 1940s or 1950s. Even in the mid-1960s, some of my talks and lectures on the merits of brief psychotherapy were received with relatively little enthusiasm. However, a number of changes have taken place in the field of psychotherapy over the past 30 years or so. One of the most interesting, and in my own view one of the most important, has been the gradual acceptance of brief and short-term forms of psychotherapy. As discussed in the text, the earlier emphasis, deriving from psychoanalysis, that effective therapy had to be long-term, has gradually given way to the reality that therapeutic change can be secured in relatively brief time. Most reports pertaining to the length of psychotherapy have indicated clearly that most of the psychotherapy conducted in the United States is of the brief variety. Furthermore, of even greater significance is that there exists now a body of research data that lends support to the claims made for the effectiveness of several forms of brief psychotherapy.

Another interesting development has also become very evident. Many psychological practitioners, for a variety of reasons, seemingly have become less doctrinaire in their approach to psychotherapy and have adopted an eclectic stance. This is also the approach I have taken to the practice of brief psychotherapy. The point of view and the procedures described in the following pages are eclectic in that they are not restricted to any single or narrow view of psychotherapy. Whatever procedures appear to fit a given case the best and have some empirical support are the procedures most likely to be used.

I will not repeat here the reasons that have led me to use the eclectic approach that I do because they are discussed later. I can simply state that both my own therapeutic experience in a variety of settings and my reading of the research literature on psychotherapy have influenced my practice. I have tried as best I can to describe in the following pages what I view as the basic features of my eclectic approach. It is my own belief that most forms of psychotherapy contain common features. These therapeutic variables, therefore, are truly important, and they receive particular emphasis in this book.

I have written this book primarily for practitioners of brief psychotherapy and counseling. I sincerely hope that it will be of some value to them. I also hope that the book will be of potential use in graduate programs that train counselors and psychotherapists.

I am indebted to the many students who have taken psychotherapy courses and practica with me over the years as well as the interns, residents, and graduate students that I have supervised in therapy. I have learned a great deal from this experience. I also want to acknowledge the outstanding typing performance of Mrs. Judith Knese, who somehow was always able to decipher my often corrected and unintelligible scribbling and to produce errorless pages of text. For her help, I am most grateful.

Sol L. Garfield

Chapter 1

Introduction: Developments in Brief Psychotherapy

The necessary or desirable length of psychotherapy has been a matter of discussion and controversy for a number of years. Although Freud tended to be somewhat defensive about the length of time required for psychoanalysis, which appeared to be 6 months to a year, there was some hope that as the method became perfected the time required might be shortened. Some of his early followers, such as Rank and Ferenczi (1925), even experimented with attempts at reducing the time required for therapy. However, in general, such attempts were not viewed too favorably by most psychoanalysts. In fact, as psychoanalysis became more popular and was being perfected, the length of time required appeared to increase, particularly in the U.S. Even 30 years ago Schmideberg (1958) remarked: "Psychoanalysis has been practiced on an increasingly large scale for the last 50 years; the length of individual treatment has become longer and longer, amounting sometimes to 5, 10 and 15 years" (p. 236).

It is only in relatively recent times that brief psychotherapy has become respectable and that one can openly admit that most psychotherapy is actually brief. The earlier dominance of psychoanalytic and related psychodynamic views concerning psychotherapy led to the expectation that effective therapy had to be of long duration. Because the personal difficulties of the patient supposedly developed over a period of many years, it was believed that a reasonably long period of time would be required in order for significant improvement to be obtained. Accompanying this view was the belief that only by helping the patient to secure insight into the unconscious conflicts causing his or

1

her difficulties could he or she be helped. Such therapeutic work, therefore, was a long-term process and could not be hurried lest the patient become overly threatened and leave therapy. Too quick an attempt at uncovering repressed material might also lead to the shattering of the patient's defenses and to possible disintegration of personality. Furthermore, if one did not get to the source of the neurotic difficulty and concentrated only on treating the symptom, the result would be the eventual appearance of substitute symptoms. This latter criticism frequently was made of behavior therapy by analytically oriented therapists, although such criticism appears to have decreased noticeably in recent years.

In short, effective therapy had to be intensive, reconstructive, and, of course, take plenty of time. Brief therapies, on the other hand, were usually referred to as supportive or directive therapies and tended to be viewed as less effective—generally, for less desirable clients. From the traditional psychodynamic point of view, the effects of such therapies were mainly palliative.

Nevertheless, despite the conventionally held views, there were some attempts made at shortening the length of psychotherapy. Following the earlier attempts by Ferenczi and Rank in the 1920s, the most notable attempt to devise an abbreviated form of psychotherapy was made by two distinguished psychoanalysts, Franz Alexander and Thomas M. French (1946). Alexander and French were the director and associate director of the Chicago Institute for Psychoanalysis. Alexander, in particular, was an outstanding advocate of attempts to reduce the length of psychotherapy and increase its efficiency. However, his work in this regard was not received favorably by his fellow analysts. Apparently, few psychoanalysts wanted the "pure gold" of psychoanalysis diluted with baser metals of briefer psychotherapy. Some of Alexander's outspoken and critical statements apparently were not what many analysts wanted to hear:

> Recently many psychoanalysts, puzzled by the great discrepancy between the length of treatment, frequency of interviews and therapeutic results, have felt the need for a thorough, critical reexamination of the therapeutic factors . . . .
>
> Occasionally one or two psychotherapeutic interviews, rich in emotional experience and insight, may have a more revelatory effect upon certain patients than months of analysis have on others. I have seen more than one patient who, under the influence of a few interviews, became sufficiently free to undertake tasks in life and to enter experiences which he never could before; and these new experiences influenced his personality as much as a long analysis in many cases. (Alexander, 1944, p. 3).

Two years later, in the introduction to *Alexander and French's, Psychoanalytic Therapy. Principles and Application* (1946), Alexander stated:

It is argued by some psychoanalysts that quick therapeutic results cannot indicate deep thoroughgoing changes in the dynamic structure of the personality, that years are required to bring about such fundamental changes. Others excuse the lack of therapeutic result in prolonged analyses by the patient's "resistance." They have comforted themselves by saying the patient is not "fully analyzed" and they are convinced that further treatment will eventually bring the desired results. Then, when results still do not come, they often take refuge in deciding that the patient is a "latent schizophrenic." (p. V)

There were also a few other publications in the 1940s that reported some attempts at modifying therapy in order to reduce its duration. For example, Frohman (1948) described his procedures in a book entitled *Brief Psychotherapy*. In general, he described a somewhat eclectic approach that was adapted to fit the requirements of the individual case. Frohman stated that his therapy usually required about 20 to 30 hours of therapy.

Another variant was offered by Herzberg in 1946. Herzberg called his approach *active psychotherapy*. One of its unusual features consisted of the therapists' prescribing certain tasks for the patient to perform. Although the therapist was called on to play an active role in this form of psychotherapy, it was believed that the patient's independence was fostered by the carrying out and completing of various tasks. The similarity between this and more recent techniques, such as behavioral rehearsal and task assignments, is readily apparent. According to Herzberg (1946), the set tasks did not allow the patient to procrastinate in therapy or to be as comfortable as he or she might be in psychoanalysis. As contrasted with the latter, the length of therapy was found to be considerably shortened.

There are other examples of modifications and approaches in psychotherapy that have gone relatively unnoticed or have received some recognition only at a later time. Reports of conditioning therapies were available in the 1920s (Franks, 1969; Yates, 1970) and in the 1940s (Salter, 1949), but apparently the zeitgeist was not conducive to a favorable response. It was only in the past 25 years that the behavior therapies have really come into their own.

Despite some of the innovative attempts described, brief psychotherapy continued to be viewed as rather superficial. However, over the past 25 years, there has been a significant change in how brief psychotherapy is perceived. No one factor can be designated clearly as causing this change. Rather, a number of events appear to have played a role in this development. Some brief mention of each of these possible influences follows.

In recent years psychotherapy has been popularized and democratized. Intensive long-term psychotherapy, however, is an expensive and demanding undertaking that is clearly not for everyone. In fact, it is for only a select few. However, as the need for psychological services became more apparent in the post-World War II period, attempts were made to modify and streamline mental health services in order to better meet the needs of large segments of our society who had been underserved previously. The report of the Joint Commission on Mental Illness and Health (1961), for example, pointed to the many inadequacies and limitations in our mental health facilities and personnel. Psychoanalysis was singled out particularly because the lengthy preparation of its practitioners and the length of time required for treatment greatly limited its impact and potential impact in terms of meeting the nation's needs. According to the Commission, "It is principally effective for a limited number of carefully selected patients who are not totally incapacitated by their illness and do not require hospitalization" (Joint Commission on Mental Illness and Health, 1961, p. 80). There clearly was a need to train additional personnel to staff the recommended and developing community mental health centers and to develop more efficient methods of treatment.

The community mental health movement in the 1960s also brought with it a number of innovative ideas such as crisis intervention, emergency clinic facilities with around-the-clock service, indigenous and paraprofessional counselors, and the like. Along with these innovative attempts at change, there also appeared a much greater emphasis on relatively brief therapy.

With the expansion of community mental health services and the increased output of a broader array of mental health workers, the clientele available for psychotherapeutic services not only increased but also changed. Psychotherapy was no longer viewed as something for "the rich or the crazy," as one popular magazine put it (Rivero, 1977). Rather, it was seen as a potential treatment modality for practically everyone, and many of the expectations that accompanied this change tended to emphasize briefer therapeutic encounters. Interestingly enough, a number of the forms of brief therapy that were developed during the 1960s utilized a psychoanalytic framework.

Bellak and Small (1965) developed a brief therapy approach that provided emergency services on an around-the-clock basis. This was done so that individuals in a crisis could obtain immediate help and avoid being put on a waiting list. There were several reasons for providing therapy at a time of crisis: (a) some individuals may be disinclined to seek help when the crisis eases; (b) the individual who is helped over the crisis situation is able more quickly to reintegrate him or herself and return to a previous level of adjustment; and (c) intervention at the time of crisis may also serve a preventative function in forestalling the emergence of a more chronic or severe pattern of adjustment.

The number of sessions used by Bellak and Small (1965) ranged from one to six. Because such therapy is quite definitely brief, the psychotherapist has to be particularly alert to the interactions with the client. He or she must quickly assess the client's strengths, weaknesses, and life situation and develop some formulation of the problem. Bellak and Small (1965) described the active role of the therapist in the following way:

> In brief psychotherapy, the therapist does not have time for insight to develop; he must foster insight. He does not have time to wait for working through, he must stimulate working through. And where these basic aspects of the therapeutic process are not forthcoming, he must invent alternatives. (p.6)

Another form of brief psychotherapy was developed by a group at the Langley Porter Neuropsychiatric Institute in San Francisco (Harris, Kalis, & Freeman, 1963, 1964; Kalis, Freeman, & Harris, 1964). As is true with most other forms of brief psychotherapy, the emphasis was on what is termed the selected focus of the therapy. Although what is viewed as the focus of therapy varies with the different approaches to brief psychotherapy, practically all of them do emphasize this aspect. One point emphasized by Harris and his colleagues (1963, 1964) was ascertaining why the patient seeks help at this particular time. The focus, therefore, was on the current crisis that interfered with the patient's usual level of functioning. Therapy also was to be provided at the time of crisis, and the active role of the therapist was stressed. Although this group of therapists did not consider brief therapy as the definitive treatment for all patients, they thought that the seven sessions or less that they provided were sufficient for perhaps two thirds of the cases they saw.

One additional form of brief analytically oriented psychotherapy can be mentioned because it differs in several ways from the two just described. This is the brief therapy developed by Sifneos (1965, 1981). This approach was developed to deal more quickly with those who had "circumscribed" neurotic difficulties and symptoms. The length of this brief therapy varies from 2 to 12 months on a weekly basis, and the therapist focuses on that area of the patient's conflicts that appear to underlie his or her symptoms. Deep-seated characterological problems, such as passivity or dependency, are avoided. Although the role of the therapist is compared to that of an unemotionally involved teacher, it is difficult to understand how a therapist can remain unemotionally involved in psychotherapy that lasts as long as 1 year. Sifneos also places considerable emphasis on the proper selection of patients, and this selective quality limits its general usefulness. Furthermore, a therapy that may last 1 year is brief only by comparison with long-term psychotherapies and would not be viewed as brief by many other individuals.

A number of other reports of brief psychotherapy also were published in the 1960s, thus indicating a growing interest in brief therapy (Haskell, Pugatch, & McNair, 1969; Jacobson, 1965; Malan, 1963; Rosenbaum, 1964; Swartz, 1969). Many of these reports also tended to emphasize the current crisis or current problems as the focal point of therapy. Some also contained a specific limit as to the length of therapy or the number of therapy sessions, and one can differentiate between time-limited therapies and brief therapies.

In general, time-limited therapies tend to be brief therapies with a specified time limit or number of therapy sessions. For example, clients are told at the beginning of therapy that therapy will terminate at a specified time, for example, by the 10th interview, or that therapy will not exceed 4 months in length. This has been the case generally in research studies comparing the effectiveness of various therapies, but some clinical and counseling centers have also used specified time limits, apparently with positive results (Jacobson, 1965; Leventhal & Weinberger, 1975; Muench, 1965; Swartz, 1969). Mann (1973, 1981) also used a 12-session limit in his work.

The main advantage claimed for the use of specific time limits in brief therapy is that both participants know at the outset that they have a specific and limited amount of time in which to obtain as much progress as possible. It is thus in their interests to use the allotted time constructively. Procrastination and aimless meandering in this type of psychotherapy are clearly counterproductive.

At the same time, many therapists may practice brief psychotherapy with no rigid or specified time limit. They may indicate a possible range of sessions or a likely termination point at the beginning of therapy so that the patient does have a reasonably clear idea of how long therapy is expected to last, and ambiguity on this matter is definitely diminished. Still other therapists may practice brief psychotherapy without mentioning any expected length of therapy simply because therapy just "seemed" to end in a relatively short time or the patient made the decision to terminate therapy.

During the sixties, a few studies were carried out that attempted to compare brief time-limited therapy with so-called time-unlimited therapy. In one series of investigations, time-limited psychotherapy was found to secure as favorable results as two types of unlimited psychotherapy (Shlien, 1957; Shlien, Mosak, & Dreikurs, 1962). In another such study, somewhat comparable findings also were secured (Muench, 1965). Thus, there were at least a few studies conducted during this period that provided some empirical support for the efficacy of brief time-limited psychotherapy, even though not a great deal of attention was paid to such findings.

THE AVNET REPORT

One additional study reported in 1965 is also worth mentioning because it reflects both the attitudes of a number of therapists toward brief therapy at that time and also provides at least some support for the clinical effectiveness of this type of psychotherapy. Avnet's report concerns a project carried out by Group Health Insurance of New York, which wa a trial project offering short-term outpatient psychiatric care to approximately 76,000 people who were already insured for other medical services. It was backed by the National Institute of Mental Health and cosponsored by the American Psychiatric Association and the National Association for Mental Health. Because psychiatric treatment traditionally is expensive, the pilot project limited treatment to 15 individual sessions, although no restrictions were placed on the psychiatrists as to the type of treatment to be offered, what kinds of patients were acceptable, and so forth.

About 2,100 members of the American Psychiatric Association in the New York area were invited to participate. About 900 did not, and they were queried concerning their reasons for not doing so. The largest number who replied gave the following types of responses: "I don't give short-term therapy"; "I do long-term psychotherapy exclusively"; "I confine my practice to those who benefit from psychotherapy, and none benefit appreciably by four months of treatment" (Avnet, 1965, p. 10). Others indicated their belief that no one could be helped in such a short time.

Although over 1,200 psychiatrists participated in the project, apparently because of their motivation to have psychiatric treatment included under medical insurance, it seemed that most of them were committed to long-term therapy and were skeptical of any short-term methods. Another indication of the psychiatrists' resistance to short-term therapy was evident in their recommendations with regard to further treatment—"for those patients who completed the allotted project treatments, the recommendation to continue was almost universal (94 percent)" (Avnet, 1965, p. 11).

In light of the foregoing, it is interesting to mention some other observations derived from the project. Apparently, about 30% of the treating psychiatrists modified their procedures in terms of getting results more quickly. They defined their goals more rapidly, modified their objectives, treated symptoms more directly, and were generally more active and directive. Some even viewed this as a learning experience and enjoyed it. It would seem, therefore, that with the right set of motivating circumstances, some therapists can become more flexible and innovative. Thus, if the programs that train psychotherapists can modify their programs to be less doctrinaire and to emphasize innovation, social awareness, and similar matters, there may be some hope for the future.

Another finding of interest in the Avnet study relates to ratings of outcome by the psychiatrists and a follow-up questionnaire that was completed by 740 patients about $2\frac{1}{2}$ years after completion of treatment. Although such subjective evaluations are, perhaps, of dubious or limited value, they have been used frequently in the past and the results are at least worth mentioning here. Eighty-one percent of the patients stated that they saw some improvement in themselves, with 17% of the patients listing themselves as recovered. The ratings by the psychiatrists were not much different. They rated 76% of the patients as improved, including 10.5% as recovered. These ratings certainly are as favorable as those reported for other and more long-term types of psychotherapy and are particularly surprising when we consider the apparent bias of the therapists against short-term psychotherapy. Thus, although the criteria of improvement leave something to be desired, they would appear to reflect at least some satisfaction on the part of the participants.

MORE RECENT DEVELOPMENTS

Since the 1960s, the field of psychotherapy has expanded greatly, and a number of new developments have occurred.One of these developments has been a marked increase in the number of different orientations or schools of psychotherapy. Along with this occurrence, there has been an evident decline in the relative popularity of psychoanalytically oriented views and a corresponding increase in eclecticism (Garfield & Kurtz, 1976; Smith, 1982). To the extent that psychoanalytic views tended to be correlated with long-term psychotherapy, this newer trend was potentially more accepting of briefer forms of psychotherapy. This was particularly true of behavior therapy, which was beginning to gain more general acceptance around the end of the 1960s. This newer emphasis on viewing and treating the patient's problem as a result of faulty learning and environmental contingencies, instead of as a symptom of a repressed conflict, was more congruent with briefer views of the psychotherapeutic change process.

Another possible factor in the gradually changing perception of the utility of briefer forms of psychotherapy was the publication of studies of premature termination and length of stay in outpatient psychotherapy. Although psychotherapists mainly discussed long-term psychotherapy and issues related to such therapy, the actual data secured from studies of patients attending outpatient clinics indicated something entirely different. In actuality, a large number of patients tended to drop out of psychotherapy early, and the actual average or median length of therapy reported for a variety of outpatient clinical settings was between six and eight sessions (Garfield, 1986). My own experience with this unexpected phenomenon may be of interest here. In 1949, I accepted a position with a VA outpatient clinic where everyone was engaged in psychoanalytically oriented psychotherapy. There was little question that everyone wanted to carry out intensive reconstructive psychotherapy wherever possible and that so-called supportive therapy was reserved for patients with "inadequate egos" and poor prognoses. Much to my surprise, I noted that some patients improved rather quickly without acquiring deep insights, and a large number terminated after a relatively small number of sessions, with or without the consent of their therapists. Because this experience was so unexpected, during a lull in our intakes I undertook a study of how many sessions of actual therapy each patient received. A colleague and I examined all the closed cases in the clinic's files, 1,216 actual cases files. Of this number, 560 patients actually began therapy. Our analysis indicated that about two-thirds of the cases received less than 10 sessions, 20% remained for 10 to 19 sessions, and 13% remained for 20 or more sessions (Garfield & Kurz, 1952). Only 7 cases received over 50 treatment sessions. Thus, in actuality, our clinic practiced brief therapy although many of my colleagues thought otherwise!

This study was conducted over 35 years ago, and since that time many additional studies have been reported with essentially comparable results (Garfield, 1986). As a consequence, the facts of early termination and the preponderance of brief therapy have become more generally known and accepted. As noted, even a variety of psychodynamically oriented forms of brief psychotherapy have appeared (Luborsky, 1984; Malan, 1963, 1976; Sifneos, 1965, 1981; Strupp & Binder, 1984), and comprehensive scholarly reviews of research on the effectiveness of brief psychotherapy have also been published (Butcher & Koss, 1978; Koss & Butcher, 1986). All of these developments clearly attest to the growing popularity of briefer forms of psychotherapy and to the increased recognition accorded such types of psychotherapy.

One recent advertisement for a conference on "Modifications of Psychoanalytic Psychotherapy" illustrates this change in point of view toward brief psychotherapy:

Many factors have forced the psychoanalytically oriented psychotherapist to modify treatment techniques, including the fiscal constraints imposed by limitations of insurance coverage and by high fees, as well as patient reticence/resistance against the commitment of time and effort for their psychotherapy. Treatment approaches have evolved which offer effective alternatives to extensive psychoanalytic psychotherapy, and this conference will consider several of these in comparison with more traditional therapy. (Program II, 6th Annual Psychotherapy Conference)

One additional and quite recent trend that is also of some importance both for research and practice in psychotherapy, is the appearance of psychotherapy manuals. These rather detailed instructions for conducting specified forms of brief psychotherapy are one means for insuring that a specific form of therapy is actually being conducted. This issue arose from past concerns pertaining to the fidelity or integrity of the psychotherapy being evaluated. These manuals, as evident in the Collaborative Study of Depression coordinated by the NIMH (National Institute of Mental Health: Elkin, Parloff, Hadley, & Autry, 1985), can be used to train and monitor the therapist's adherence to the particular forms of psychotherapy being studied. In the case of the two psychotherapies evaluated in the Collaborative Study, Cognitive-Behavioral Therapy (Beck, Rush, Shaw, & Emery, 1979) and Interpersonal Psychotherapy (Klerman, Weissman, Rounsaville, & Chevron, 1984), both were brief forms of psychotherapy requiring 16 sessions of therapy. In addition to the fact that brief therapies lend themselves more readily to research appraisals than indeterminate therapies and consequently were used in the Collaborative Study, the results secured also provide some support for their effectiveness.

Consequently, brief psychotherapies now are widely used and their popularity has grown in recent years. Beyond such a testimonial, it can be stressed also that considerably more research evaluations, and of distinctly better quality, have been conducted on brief forms of psychotherapy than on longer forms of therapy. The research evidence not only points to moderate levels of efficacy for many brief forms of psychotherapy, but comparative studies of brief and relatively longer forms of psychotherapy have not demonstrated any clear superiority of the latter (Koss & Butcher, 1986). Consequently, individuals who practice mainly brief psychotherapy need have no feelings of inadequacy. As far as can be ascertained at present, brief forms of psychotherapy are the most efficient forms and are at least as effective as other forms of psychotherapy for most patients.

GOALS AND OBJECTIVES OF BRIEF PSYCHOTHERAPY

It is often stated that the goals and objectives of different forms of psychotherapy differ rather markedly. Psychoanalysis, for example, tends to play down the value of symptom amelioration and instead emphasizes the matter of significant personality change. Thus, most psychoanalysts have tended to view therapies, such as behavior therapy, that are mainly concerned with behavioral or symptomatic change as limited. In a related manner, as we have noted, practitioners and proponents of long-term psychotherapy tend to view brief forms of psychotherapy as rather superficial or lesser forms of therapy. On the other hand, as indicated earlier, I and a number of others believe that brief therapies are the treatments of choice for most patients with psychological problems who have the potential for being helped by means of psychotherapy. For my point of view, long-term psychotherapy is actually a less preferred form of psychological therapy as far as most people are concerned. It is more costly, requires a much greater period of time, and the results have not been demonstrated to be superior to briefer forms of therapy.

The general goal of brief psychotherapy is to help the client overcome the problems or discomforts that lead him or her to seek out someone for psychotherapeutic help. Relief of pain, discomfort, or unhappiness are what the client seeks and hopes to receive from therapy. It is important that we as therapists respect these goals and not try to substitute other goals of our own. Helping the client to be rid of discomforts and to function at a reasonably adequate level are quite desirable goals. One need not strive for some mythical state of personality transformation, even though some such happenings apparently do occur in accounts of religious conversions and related experiences. As Colby (1951) stated, "a psychotherapist should not expect great transformations equivalent to a psychological rebirth or a complete reorganization of the patient's personality. . . . Psychotherapy is repair work" (p. 3). Colby was not limiting his statements to brief psychotherapy but was writing about psychotherapy in general. Furthermore, satisfactory and economical repair work is not to be belittled, even though the comparison may not be the best one for psychotherapy. If attention in therapy can also be devoted to the development of coping skills and the possible prevention of future individual upset, then therapy may even go beyond repair work.

Thus, if at all possible, an auxiliary goal of brief psychotherapy should be the development of coping skills in order that the individual may become better able to handle and prevent future problems. Traditional dynamic psychotherapy emphasized the importance of insight as the main therapeutic variable in facilitating positive outcome. The implication was that once the individual understood the repressed unconscious conflict that produced his or her symptoms, the latter would gradually disappear. However, intellectual understanding or insight alone was not necessarily curative, as many analysts later noted. The client also needs to change his or her perceptions of environmental stimuli in a manner congruent with better adjustment and also develop new behav iors that allow him or her to overcome past and future obstacles to better mental health.

Consequently, helping the client to overcome his or her problems and to be able to handle future difficulties in a more constructive manner are the primary goals or objectives of brief psychotherapy. The therapy is of necessity problem-oriented and directive. In terms of directiveness, two distinct aspects can be differentiated. On a theoretical or schematic level, the therapy is directive in the sense that attention is focused from the start on the patient's problems and the current situation—the here and now as contrasted with the then and there. The patient's present thoughts and behaviors are dealt with in a direct fashion and not indirectly. From the standpoint of the therapist's role or behavior, brief therapy is also quite directive, particularly when compared with psychoanalytic psychotherapy or with client-centered psychotherapy. The therapist both directs and is an active participant in brief psychotherapy; this would be true for most forms of brief psychotherapy, not just the one described here.

The specificity of the goals of brief therapy, the active role of the therapist, and the expectations concerning the length of therapy all help to facilitate the process of therapy and to avoid some of the pitfalls that occur in long-term psychotherapy. As Mann (1973) pointed out, long-term psychotherapy as generally practiced has certain features that tend to prolong the duration of therapy unduly and create an undesirable dependency on the part of both participants:

> It has long been my conviction that long-term psychotherapy with insufficiently or inaccurately defined treatment goals leads to a steady widening of and diffusion of content. This creates a growing sense of ambiguity in the mind of the therapist as to what he is about, and, while it may affect the patient similarly, it surely increases the patient's dependence on the therapist. The result is that patient and therapist come to need each other, so that bringing the case to a conclusion seems impossible. Since treatment is the responsibility of the therapist, the problem of excessively long treatment lies in the domain of the therapist and not the patient. Further, it has been my position that the constant exposure to large doses of severe psychopathology that is a rather natural consequence of training programs in psychiatry tends to diminish the young therapist's peripheral vision, so to speak, so that he is unable to appreciate the assets of the patient before him. He tends to develop very little confidence in his patient's ability, capacity, and motivation to help himself. It is a short step then to being convinced that no patient can long survive without his close and indefinitely prolonged attention. (p. $\bar{X}$)

The practice of brief psychotherapy thus differs in many important respects from the practice of the more traditional long-term psychotherapy. Having delineated these differences, let us now turn to the matter of who may profit from receiving brief psychotherapy.

WHO MAY PROFIT FROM BRIEF PSYCHOTHERAPY

Having offered some general statements about the overall goals or objectives of brief psychotherapy, it is worth illustrating these general statements with some more concrete details and examples. Obviously, the problems that the client has and for which he or she seeks treatment have to be problems that are potentially helped by means of brief psychotherapy. The latter is by no means a panacea for all human ills. Rather, such therapy is potentially helpful for selected psychological problems. In a general way, I would exclude very serious disorders such as psychoses, so-called borderline disorders, addictions, and the like. Many of these disorders do not respond well to psychotherapy alone, regardless of the length of treatment. However, a variety of conditions in which anxiety or depression are important features can be helped by means of brief psychotherapy. It is not necessary to be overly selective in terms of clients and to restrict treatment to only a limited number of diagnostic categories or personality types. Sifneos (1965, 1981), for example, is quite selective in the patients he deems suitable for his form of short-term anxiety-provoking psychotherapy. Among other criteria, he includes a history of "meaningful" interpersonal relationships, above-average intelligence and psychological sophistication, and a high degree of motivation for change. Such selectivity would appear to screen out a very large number of individuals who need and seek out psychotherapeutic help. Although such selectivity may make the task of psychotherapy less difficult or more enjoyable for the therapist, it would seemingly cater to those with somewhat minimal problems.

With the exception of the very seriously disturbed individuals mentioned earlier, brief therapy can be considered for most patients who are in touch with reality, are experiencing some discomfort, and have made the effort to seek help for their difficulties. Several of the psychodynamic approaches to brief therapy emphasize that there should be a focal problem or specific focus for the therapy. Although the theoretical rationale for this is that in brief or time-limited therapy only a limited goal is possible, I would concur that brief therapy should be focused therapy. In fact, all psychotherapy should be focused therapy and focused on the problems of the patient. Although unwarranted meandering in therapy is usually inefficient and ineffective, one need not be unduly restrictive. The client may start out in therapy with what appears to be his or her main problem, but as therapy progresses another problem may appear and become the central focus. The therapist, of course, has to evaluate the significance of what occurs in psychotherapy and guide the therapeutic process accordingly. However, the problems a patient has are not completely separate and disconnected. Rather, they are interrelated manifestations of less than adequate adjustment in one human being, and in one sense the therapist is dealing with one problem—the problem that a particular individual is having in his or her life situation at a particular time.

Several therapists, in agreement with the views presented here, take a more liberal view of who can profit from brief psychotherapy. In one of the earlier books on brief psychotherapy, Wolberg (1965) went so far as to say that: "The best strategy, in my opinion, is to assume that every patient, irrespective of diagnosis, will respond to short-term treatment unless he proves himself refractory to it" (p. 140). According to Wolberg, if the patient does not respond to brief therapy, then the therapist "can always resort to prolonged therapy" (p. 140). In a similar vein, Harris, Kalis, and Freeman (1964) did not consider brief therapy as the definitive treatment for all patients. However, they felt that it seemed a worthwhile therapeutic intake procedure for most patients, and that for a large number it actually enabled them to get back to a reasonable level of functioning in a short time. Where brief therapy was not really successful, it still was of value in clarifying the patients' problems and motivation for therapy, and thus was potentially useful for whatever additional therapy was undertaken.

Both of the aforementioned viewpoints were novel and pioneering expositions when published a quarter of a century ago. They advocated a wider usage of brief psychotherapy but still indicated some recourse to long-term psychotherapy when and if brief psychotherapy failed. The implied assumption in such statements appears to be that long-term psychotherapy will remedy the failure that occurred in brief therapy. This is clearly an assumption that does not appear to have strong empirical support. As Budman and Gurman (1983) pointed out, "to assume that a particular patient has failed at brief therapy because of a poor response to a trial of such treatment and now has no alternative other than long-term therapy fails to take into account a variety of other alternatives" (p. 287). Among the other possibilities they mention are a change of therapists, the type of treatment, the duration of sessions, the between-visits intervals, and the like.

At the present time, it does appear as if brief psychotherapy is generally considered a suitable form of psychotherapy for most of the patients referred for psychotherapy. Some practitioners, such as Sifneos (1981) and Malan (1963, 1976), who have set up entrance requirements for admission to brief psychotherapy, have utilized trial periods of therapy or more detailed evaluation of prospective patients. As already indicated, aside from the exceptions noted, there is really no clear need for such selection and exclusiveness. Most patients will respond as effectively to brief psychotherapy as they will to psychotherapy that continues for several years. In fact, most patients clearly prefer briefer forms of therapy, and reports of various studies of the length of psychotherapy support their preference. Most of the psychotherapy conducted in the United States is brief if we define brief therapy as consisting of up to 20 to 25 sessions (Garfield, 1986; Howard, Kopata, Krause, & Orlinsky, 1986). According to Koss and Butcher (1986), "The clinical literature on brief psychotherapy is quite consistent in considering a 25-session contact as the upper limit of a brief treatment" (p. 629). Although there may not be complete unanimity in specifying the exact limits of brief psychotherapy, most individuals would agree that therapy that lasts 5 years is not brief.

The Role of the Therapist

Although there is some variation among how therapists tend to function in brief psychotherapy, there are certain general characteristics that appear to be common for most. Perhaps the most common pertains to the activity of the therapist. In brief psychotherapy, the therapist is usually an active participant. If the time is to be used effectively and efficiently, the therapist cannot sit back and simply be a passive participant. Rather, he or she must guide the therapeutic process in terms of the desired goals and objectives of the therapy. Although the client is also expected to be an active participant, the therapist participates actively and sees to it that the time is used as constructively as possible.

In part because forms of psychotherapy vary and also because therapists as individuals vary in how they conduct therapy, there is no precise or quantitative estimate of how active the therapist must be. The point can only be made in a general way that the therapist cannot be a passive participant or observer. The therapist also must have a strongly held view that brief therapy is a worthwhile and desirable endeavor. The therapist's confidence in his or her therapy is a common therapeutic variable in all forms of therapy, and this is certainly true in brief psychotherapy. A psychotherapist who views brief psychotherapy as a less desirable form of psychotherapy and who consents to use it because a particular client cannot afford long-term psychotherapy is likely to be less successful. Clients are particularly sensitive to communications from the therapist that pertain to the therapy and themselves. They are quick to pick up attitudes reflecting doubts about the treatment or the client, a lack of confidence on the part of the therapist, and the like. Thus, the therapist needs to be both confident and realistic about what the therapy can offer and about the prospects for change for the particular client.

The emphasis on the active role of the therapist does not mean that the therapist must always be verbally active, offering interpretations and direction ad infinitum. I have supervised at least a few students who confused the quantity of their own verbal output with the quality of the ongoing psychotherapy. The activity of the therapist pertains to the overall role of the therapist. Because time is important, the therapist has to plan his or her activities carefully, lead or direct sessions so that the necessary objectives are obtained, constantly evaluate how therapy is progressing, consider what changes need to be made, plan homework assignments, and the like. In fact, it can be argued that the therapist has to be even more sensitive and responsive to the behavorial and other cues of the patient in brief therapy than longer forms of therapy, because each session constitutes a significant portion of the therapy.

A humorous story recounted in the paper by Budman and Gurman (1983) to illustrate the difference in the role of the therapist in brief therapy as contrasted with longer-term psychotherapy is worth quoting here:

> Additionally, the effective brief therapist cannot remain detached and uninvolved, since activity and planning are two of the central character- istics of brief treatment. The often told joke goes that when the young analyst and the old analyst met on their way out of their respective offices, the young analyst was amazed at how fresh and alert the old analyst appeared (compared to his own exhaustion). He said to him: "Dr. Von Klopfer, how is it that you always appear so chipper after hearing people's problems all day?" Dr. Von Klopfer replied, "Who listens?" Not listening is not a response available to the effective brief therapist. (p. 288)

In general then, the therapist conducting brief psychotherapy knows in advance that he or she has a limited amount of time in which to work therapeutically. Each session, therefore, must be used as constructively as possible. In the process, the therapist must also try to engage the patient as soon as possible as an active partner in order that progress can be made. In order for events to proceed satisfactorily, the therapist has to communicate both her or his desire to help the patient and his or her competence to do so. An active therapist communicates these features much more successfully to most patients than does a passive therapist who just listens. This does not mean that the effective therapist is not a good listener. Rather, it means that such a therapist is more than just a good listener.

In their excellent review chapter on research on brief psychotherapy, Koss and Butcher (1986) describe the active role of the therapist in the following succinct manner: "Generally, being 'active' means talking more, directing the conversation when necessary, actively exploring areas of interest, offering support and guidance, formulating plans of action for the patient to follow, assigning homework, teaching problem solving, and encouraging a constructive life philosophy" (p. 643).

Clearly, there are many different types of activities that the therapist will be engaged in over the course of therapy. The frequency of use of some procedures will be determined by the individual preferences and beliefs of the therapist and by the specific needs of the individual client. The more eclectic the therapist, the more likely that there will be a wide range of therapist activities.

Before concluding our introductory remarks about brief psychotherapy, some additional comments should be made. There are a number of reasons that brief therapies measured in weeks would naturally be preferred over longer-term therapies that tend to be measured in years. At least from the client's or patient's point of view, brief therapy has a number of advantages. The quickest alleviation of the client's distress and discomfort is clearly the most preferred. It is also evident that brief therapy should cost the least amount of money and interfere the least with the client's daily living. Thus, it would seem as if most individuals would prefer the most efficient, economical, and least intrusive form of psychotherapy—and this would appear to be true for the great majority of people. On the other hand, it it only fair to point out that there are some clients and therapists who still favor long-term psychotherapy. Such persons, a minority in my opinion, favor more traditional views and tend to see brief therapies as superficial or supportive. Different goals are emphasized for long-term intensive reconstructive psychotherapy as compared with briefer therapies. Significant personality change is claimed for the former and only symptomatic treatment for the latter. How well or how frequently significant personality change is actually secured by means of long-term psychotherapy is by no means clear, because adequate research studies are an endangered species. However, as discussed in Chapter 9, there is a moderate amount of empirical support for brief forms of psychotherapy.

Thus, as indicated, there are clients, as well as therapists, who favor long-term psychodynamic therapy and seek out such therapy. Many of these persons come from the mental health professions, some essentially want to understand themselves as fully as possible, some have had previous therapy of one sort or another, and some have read about Freud and the contributions of psychoanalysis. However, it is extremely doubtful if more than a very small percentage of people require or would profit from long-term psychotherapy. In the Harvard Community Health Plan it has been estimated that no more than 1% to 2% of their population would require long-term psychotherapy (Bennett & Wisneski, 1979). Koss (1979), in a study of clients seen in private practice, also questioned the view that long-term psychotherapy was the treatment of choice for "verbal, mild to moderately disturbed persons" (p. 211).

A fairly convincing case, therefore, can be made for brief psychotherapy as the preferred treatment for most of the patients with mild to moderate degrees of disturbance who seek out or are referred for outpatient psychotherapy. This has always been the situation in reality, although it has not been fully acknowledged until recently. However, the current emphasis on both accountability and third-party payments has made practitioners more receptive and accepting of brief forms of psychotherapy.

What follows in the subsequent pages is an eclectic presentation of brief psychotherapy as practiced by the author. The potential strengths and limitations of an eclectic approach to psychotherapy will not be debated here. I have made such a presentation elsewhere (Garfield, 1980), and additional discussions are available in the work of others (Norcross, 1986). It is sufficient to say that my views are representative of most psychotherapists, to the extent that most tend to identify themselves as eclectics. Calling oneself an eclectic, of course, does not really identify the actual therapeutic practice in which one is engaged. It simply means that the individual does not limit him or herself to one theoretical orientation. Whatever is considered potentially useful can and will be used. In the pages that follow, techniques and concepts from several different orientations are described and a justification for their use provided. Wherever possible, recourse to empirical research data is made.

Chapter 2

An Overview of Possible Therapeutic Variables

One of the interesting, and also perplexing, aspects of psychotherapy is the great diversity of different schools and orientations that currently exist in this field. This growth and proliferation of therapeutic approaches has been most marked in the past 20 to 30 years. In the mid-1960s, for example, I collected my own list of over 60 different approaches to psychotherapy and thought this was an amazing phenomenon. A few years later, a report of the Research Task Force of the National Institute of Mental Health (1975) mentioned that there were over 130 different types of psychotherapy. Just 5 years later, Herink (1980) published his account of over 200 different forms of psychotherapy, and more recently Kazdin (1986) referred to a statement of over 400 different techniques. Needless to say, if this rate of increase continues, at some point we will have a different form of psychotherapy for every person in the United States. This manifestation of the free enterprise system, perhaps, may epitomize true democracy, but whether it is an ideal situation for psychotherapy is another matter.

Although one is tempted to list a number of the various approaches to psychotherapy in order to illustrate this diversity, I forego this temptation and instead discuss some of the implications this has for the psychotherapist. In this process I refer to a few of the better-known approaches to psychotherapy.

Three well-known and quite distinct orientations in psychotherapy are psychoanalysis, behavior therapy, and Rogerian or client-centered therapy. In terms of both theoretical orientation and therapeutic procedures or techniques, these forms of psychotherapy differ noticeably. In psychoanalytically oriented forms of psychotherapy, there is an emphasis on the importance of the client's early life experience, on repressed and unconscious conflicts, on the transference relationship that develops in therapy, and on the client's resistance to the therapeutic endeavor.

In order to overcome the client's resistance, the therapist relies on appropriate interpretations of the unconscious dynamic conflicts. Over time, the client is thought to gain insight into these symptom-producing conflicts, and as a result their negative influence gradually lessens. The particular relationship developed in therapy and the therapist's interpretations of the client's behavior are key elements in the therapeutic process.

In client-centered psychotherapy, the conceptualization of the therapeutic process, the theoretical view of personality, and the nature of the therapist-client relationship differ quite noticeably from the psychoanalytic view. In client-centered therapy, the emphasis is on the need for congruence between the self and the person's experience and on the therapeutic conditions of empathy, nonpossessive warmth, and genuineness on the part of the therapist as necessary and sufficient for client change. The client is viewed as having the potential for positive change, and the therapist's role is less directive. The therapist attempts to reflect the client's feelings and to avoid offering interpretations.

Behavior therapy, on the other hand, has traditionally stressed principles of classical and operant conditioning. There is no emphasis on unconscious repressed conflicts or on the importance of very early childhood experiences in the etiology of behavioral disorders. Instead, environmental contingencies, schedules of reinforcement, and the actual performance of the client in therapy and outside the therapy situation are highlighted. More recently, there has also been an emphasis on social learning and cognitive restructuring.

Even from these brief descriptions, it is evident that these three psychotherapeutic orientations differ quite markedly in their main theoretical emphases. To some extent also, the role of the therapist in conducting these different forms of psychotherapy also would appear to differ noticeably. In fact, studies comparing some of these forms of psychotherapy have indicated that the therapists conducting these therapies can be differentiated reliably. In the well-known study by Sloane and his colleagues, psychoanalytically oriented therapists and behavior therapists were identified as utilizing procedures associated with their respective orientations (Sloane, Staples, Cristol, Yorkston, & Whipple, 1975). Similar results have been reported for the NIMH Treatment for Depression Collaborative Study comparing cognitive therapy and interpersonal therapy (DeRubeis, Hollon, Evans, & Bemis, 1982).

On the basis of such results it seems clear that therapists representing different schools of psychotherapy function in different ways that can be identified as representative of the specific schools—or at least this is the case when individuals are selected or trained to represent different orientations in research investigations. Yet despite these apparent differences in therapist behaviors and therapeutic procedures, roughly comparable results have been obtained in the majority of comparative studies and reviews (Bergin & Lambert, 1978; Garfield, 1983b; Lambert, Shapiro, & Bergin, 1986; Smith, Glass, & Miller, 1980). Furthermore, although only a small number of the several hundred different forms of psychotherapy have actually been evaluated in a systematic manner, if comparisons of all the therapies produced similar results, it would indeed be difficult to explain the findings.

If the various forms of psychotherapy do differ in procedures and theory as much as they appear to, how can we explain that the differences in outcome are so small? This is an intriguing question that has never really been answered. However, it does deserve some thought on the part of psychotherapists, and I come back to this issue later in this chapter. For now, it is sufficient to recognize that there are many very different forms of psychotherapy and that they all claim to be effective forms of treatment. Furthermore, each seems to emphasize some components of human functioning as the main variables or ingredients in their form of psychotherapy. Thus, some emphasize the awareness of repressed conflicts and the attainment of insight, some stress the importance of the therapeutic relationship, and others focus on behaviors and cognitions. How individual therapists choose a particular orientation is an interesting issue in its own right, but we do not discuss it here. Instead, we examine another interesting development in psychotherapy that is precisely the opposite of the proliferation of orientations in psychotherapy.

Eclecticism and Eclectic Approaches

At the same time that the number of psychotherapeutic approaches has increased tremendously, the number of individuals who have identified themselves as eclectics has also grown. For example, in a survey of clinical psychologists conducted by Kelly (1961), approximately 40% identified themselves as eclectics—that is, they did not adhere to one orientation exclusively. A later survey of a similar sample by Garfield and Kurtz (1976) found that 55% of the clinical psychologists selected eclectic as their preferred orientation. More recently, Smith (1982), in a study of counseling and clinical psychologists, reported that over 41% of his sample claimed to be eclectics. Thus, although a record number of schools of psychotherapy exist, the most popular theoretical orientation appears to be eclecticism.

Although one may learn or practice primarily one orientation during graduate or professional training, at some point individuals seem to want to broaden their views of the psychotherapeutic process and to use techniques or procedures from other orientations. When they do this, they essentially become eclectic psychotherapists. Although individuals may have different reasons for using an eclectic approach, I hypothesize that most persons move in this direction in order to improve their therapeutic effectiveness. They may find that their original approach did not work as effectively as expected, or that it seems to work well with some patients but not with others. Consequently, therapists begin to modify their procedures, to add some new techniques, compare notes with other therapists, and gradually to exhibit a greater range of therapeutic activities. Admittedly, there is less security in leaving or departing from a given theoretical system that is internally consistent and provides some frame of reference as a guide for the therapist. However, eclectic therapists state that a flexible approach allows them to adapt to the needs of individual patients more readily. One adapts the approach to the patient rather than requiring the patient to adapt to the particular therapeutic approach.

At the same time, it is evident that not all eclectic psychotherapists function in the same way. In fact, on the basis of a study of 154 eclectics, it was apparent that the eclectic designation covers a fairly wide range of therapeutic views, some of which appear to be the opposite of others (Garfield & Kurtz, 1977). It was actually difficult to categorize the responses of the sample studied. However, for the largest group, the eclectic clinical psychologist is defined as using whatever theory or method seems best for the individual client. Thus, the eclectic therapist selects procedures in terms of the client and his or her problems rather than as a result of adherence to a specific theoretical view.

The implication of this survey of eclectic psychologists is that no one therapeutic system fits all psychotherapy clients. Consequently, the psychotherapist must select and adapt procedures and techniques that he or she feels will work best with specific clients. Based on our knowledge of individual differences, this certainly seems very reasonable. However, this is easier said than done. Clients can be categorized in many ways. They can be differentiated in terms of age, sex, education, socioeconomic status, type of presenting problem, severity of disturbance, social skills, interest in psychotherapy, ability to relate to others, and the like. They can also be diagnosed in terms of the current psychiatric classification system. In terms of the latter, certain procedures such as systematic desensitization or exposure in vivo may be preferred treatments or techniques for individuals suffering from agoraphobia. For other disorders, however, many different therapeutic approaches appear to be equally effective, and as yet there is no clear basis for choosing one over the others. Furthermore, whereas some therapists may be guided in their work primarily by psychiatric diagnosis, others feel that such a categorization is too gross and pay more attention to the personal qualities of the client.

Such variability among both clients and therapists indicates that precise prescriptions for conducting psychotherapy are not easy to come by, particularly among eclectics. Some will simply tell you that they apply whatever formulations or techniques seem "just right" for a given client, without really being able to spell this out in any detail. Others may appear to have a more definitive or explicit eclectic approach, as in the following example from Garfield and Kurtz (1977): "Different strokes for different folks. Learning theory to influence behavioral problems. Psychodynamic approach to motivational conflicts. Group process orientation to people with interpersonal difficulties" (p. 80). Still others emphasize mainly that they use whatever method works, and that "being a clinician almost requires some eclecticism" (Garfield & Kurtz, 1977, p. 81).

I am inclined to agree with the last statement, although many clinicians may not. Some prefer to be identified with a specific theoretical orientation, because they fully accept the rationale provided and there is a certain security in adhering to one system. However, therapists may function in ways that are not really central to their approach or use procedures or emphases that receive little formal recognition. In other words, what a psychotherapist says he or she does, and what he or she actually does may differ widely. Furthermore, variables that are emphasized by a particular therapeutic approach may not be as significant therapeutically as variables that are not emphasized. For example, several observers observed Joseph Wolpe and Arnold Lazarus work with patients for a period of 5 days and then offered their comments: "Perhaps the most striking impression we came away with was of how much use behavior therapists make of suggestion and of how much the patient's expectations and attitudes are manipulated" (Klein, Dittman, Parloff, & Gill, 1969, p. 262). The observers also stressed the important discrepancies between the theoretical postulates of behavior therapy and the actual implementation of the therapy in the real clinical situation.

Thus it is possible that even noneclectics may behave at times in an eclectic manner and use procedures not identified with their particular approach. There is nothing wrong with this as long as the therapist is aware of what he or she is doing and has a reasonable rationale for it. If not, the therapist will not be fully informed as to what is occurring and what variables are actually having a therapeutic impact. This, of course, may also occur with eclectic psychotherapists, but they are (or should be) more sensitive to the use of a variety of therapeutic procedures.

Although the potentially greater flexibility of an eclectic approach would appear to be particularly well-suited to brief psychotherapy, there have not been many descriptions published of such an approach. Surprisingly, in the review prepared by Koss and Butcher (1986), there are noticeably more psychodynamically oriented, cognitive-behavioral, and crisis-oriented brief therapies than eclectic brief therapies. On the other hand, some of the therapies that are designated as cognitive-behavioral are rather broad-ranging therapies that resemble so-called eclectic therapies. There is no need, however, to enter into a semantic controversy here. I favor an eclectic approach that seeks to adapt therapy to the particular needs of a specific client and accepts that, with very few exceptions, no one therapeutic system appears to be clearly superior to the others. I also have come to the view, alluded to earlier, that variables of consequence in psychotherapy have been frequently overlooked in the formal systems developed by the leaders of the various schools of psychotherapy. Furthermore, because of the comparability of results secured when different psychotherapies have been compared, it seems plausible to also hypothesize that a number of common therapeutic variables or factors operate in most of the psychotherapies and account for a significant portion of the positive results secured.

POTENTIAL COMMON
AND SPECIFIC THERAPEUTIC
FACTORS

Before discussing possible common therapeutic factors in psychotherapy, I provide some brief rationale for this view. It did not originate with me but for over 30 years I have been trying to draw attention to it (Garfield, 1957, 1974, 1980). One can begin by focusing on the finding that supposedly very different forms of psychotherapy, such as psychoanalytically oriented brief therapy and behavior therapy, have secured comparable outcomes (Sloane et al., 1975). Is it understandable that two approaches, so different in theory and in procedures, can secure equally positive results? Or, is it possible that there are certain common factors operating in both that actually play an important role in the results obtained?

Although the two different types of therapy could be reliably differentiated in the Sloane et al. (1975) study, commonalities could also be identified if one went beyond differences. In both instances, we have a troubled patient who has sought treatment, highly trained therapists who, despite differences in orientation, express an interest in the patient, secure information from the patient, attempt some problem formulation and treatment plan, listen to the patient, answer questions, offer encouragement, provide some explanations, and the like. Thus, if we look beyond the differences, even on a somewhat superficial level we can note similarities and commonalities. We can also note potentially significant commonalities by penetrating beneath the surface aspects of the different psychotherapies.

The Therapeutic Relationship

One feature that is common to all forms of psychotherapy is the therapeutic relationship. Although an obvious feature, the therapeutic relationship has been strongly emphasized by some orientations and has received comparatively little formal attention from others. Without question, a positive therapeutic relationship is an important requirement for a successful outcome in psychotherapy, and this applies to all forms of psychotherapy. A good therapeutic relationship may not insure a successful outcome by itself, but it is necessary if such an outcome is to be secured. If for whatever reason the patient has a negative view of the therapist, it is likely that therapy will be prematurely terminated by the patient's withdrawal from therapy or that little progress will be made. In practically all forms of therapy, the patient's active participation and cooperation are essential for a successful outcome. In fact, this matter has been emphasized in terms of both medical and psychological therapies in recent discussions of treatment compliance. If the patient does not keep his or her appointments or comply with the requirements of the treatment program, the likelihood of significant improvement is diminished.

A good relationship between therapist and patient, therefore, is an important requirement for progress in all forms of psychotherapy. Even behavior therapists, who have been viewed by some as emphasizing techniques to the exclusion of other aspects of therapy, have unequivocally affirmed the importance of a good patient-therapist relationship. According to O'Leary and Wilson (1987), "Behavior therapists attach considerable importance to the therapeutic relationship, although the social learning or behavioral conceptualization of this relationship differs from the traditional psychodynamic perspective" (pp. 383–384).

Although most psychotherapists would agree that a good client-therapist relationship is important for satisfactory progress in psychotherapy, there may not be complete agreement on how such a relationship is secured or on what factors play a role in facilitating such a relationship. It does seem evident, however, that both clients and therapists vary in a number of ways, and that these differences, in varying combinations, undoubtedly play a role in how the relationship develops.

Certain aspects do appear to be of some importance. One such aspect is how each of the participants views the other. If, for example, the therapist deviates too far from the client's expectations about how a therapist is supposed to function, does not inspire confidence in the client concerning the therapist's skills and competence, or seems to show little interest in the client's problems, the chances for a good therapeutic relationship seem unlikely. In a similar way, if the therapist perceives the client as unmotivated, hostile, critical, and devoid of most human virtues, the likelihood of developing a satisfactory relationship, one that can provide a basis for positive change, seems equally unlikely. Thus, regardless of the therapist's orientation, the way the client and therapist perceive each other is important for the kind of relationship that may develop.

Because clients differ widely in most respects, it is obvious that the therapist must respond in different but appropriate ways to each client. With some the therapist may listen more and with others talk more. With some there is a quick feeling of rapport; with others there appears to be an aloofness or a barrier preventing attachment and a positive response. In fact, if the therapist responds quite negatively to the client for whatever reason, the chances for developing a positive therapeutic relationship are slim. This would also appear to limit the opportunity for securing a positive therapeutic outcome. Consequently, the therapist must make a decision concerning whether or not he or she can develop a satisfactory working relationship with the client. If the judgment is negative, then the proper decision, professionally and ethically, is not to accerpt the client for therapy. Problems and related issues of this kind are discussed in Chapter 4. Here, the focus is primarily on the therapeutic relationship as an important variable in psychotherapy.

Although the relationship in psychotherapy has characteristics that are similar to other dyadic relationships, it also has features that are unique. There is a specified regular time for the dyad to meet and there is a very specific purpose for the meeting of the two individuals. A considerable amount of the time spent in the relationship is devoted to discussions of the feelings, thoughts, and behavior of one of the individuals, the client. Furthermore, the therapeutic relationship is (or should be) characterized by trust and confidentiality. As the client comes to trust the therapist fully, he or she can reveal previously undisclosed disturbing thoughts and feelings. In this context, the client is more able to face the negative aspects of self and to be open to the comments, suggestions, and explanations of the therapist.

There are related aspects of the relationship in psychotherapy that I have described elsewhere as follows (Garfield, 1980):

> To a certain extent, because of the relationship which has developed, the therapist may function as an agent of persuasion or reinforcement for the patient. The patient may be willing to attempt changes because of the support provided by the therapist or, in some instances, in order to please the therapist. Although the latter instance may not be viewed too positively by some therapeutic orientations, it may be a more adequate occurrence when viewed from a learning theory orientation. For example, if the client is motivated to try out some behavior which he previously avoided and sees that no negative consequences follow this behavior, he is more likely to continue with this positive behavior (p. 97).

A positive relationship in therapy, therefore, appears to increase the therapist's influence on the client. Suggestions, interpretations, homework assignments, and other activities of the therapist are more likely to be accepted and complied with than if such a relationship did not exist. Also, when a good therapeutic relationship exists, the client is more likely to model him or herself after the therapist and to take on the values of the therapist. Obviously, if the therapist is a good model, this kind of identification may have a positive impact on the client. If the therapist, unfortunately, is a poor model, the consequences may be less positive or even harmful. The psychotherapist clearly has important responsibilities in working with disturbed individuals who seek his or her help.

The therapeutic relationship is thus a variable of basic importance in psychotherapy and plays an important role in the type of outcome that is secured. The therapist must be sensitive to the way the client responds to him or her, as well as how he or she reacts to the client. A good relationship increases both the cooperation of the client and the potential positive influence of the therapist.

The therapeutic relationship is further discussed later. It is sufficient here to point out that it is a variable or aspect of psychotherapy that is common to most forms of psychotherapy, regardless of theoretical orientation. It is also a variable of consequence, and therefore it warrants the therapist's serious attention. This is particularly true in brief therapy where only a limited time is available for therapeutic work.

Interpretation, Insight, and Understanding

Another feature common to most forms of psychotherapy pertains to the increased understanding the client secures about self and personal difficulties (Garfield, 1980). Psychodynamic therapists emphasize interpretations offered by the therapist to aid the client in securing insight into repressed conflicts and in understanding the transference phenomena. Even within the psychodynamic frame of reference, there are differences in what the true insights are. Followers of Freud, Adler, Jung, Horney, and Sullivan may all look for different insights and understandings. Cognitive and behavioral therapists may operate differently but also provide explanations of a different sort to their clients. Rational-emotive therapists, for example, will point out the irrational thoughts clients have been using as potential causes of their problems, and behavior therapists, perhaps more indirectly, will also provide explanations or interpretations based on theories of learning.

This phenomenon is interesting. Various and diverse explanations or therapeutic rationales (Frank, 1971) are provided patients, and they presumably have a positive therapeutic effect. It does not seem to matter what the explanation, interpretation, or rationale is as long as the therapist presents it in a confident and knowledgeable manner and the patient accepts it as meaningful. I regard this as an important feature of psychotherapy that is common to all the therapies. However, I am also aware that this view is not readily accepted by many psychotherapists. In the first place, it appears to demean the therapist's belief in a particular theoretical view, the attainment of which has required considerable hard work and study on the part of the therapist. Second, it appears to convey a rather cavalier attitude toward all theoretical orientations in psychotherapy. And, third, it seems to imply that anything that the therapist says is equally therapeutic. This, in particular, seems very unprofessional and practically suggestive of quackery. Although it is easily understandable why many therapists would respond in this fashion, it is unfortunate. In actuality, there is an important therapeutic principle to be grasped here. It pertains to the importance of meaning, not only for the patient, but also for the therapist.

The good therapist, for the most part, develops a rationale for how he or she conducts therapy with a specific patient. In one situation, he or she may believe that the patient should be challenged or confronted; in another situation the therapist may deliberately avoid such a direct approach. The therapist in both situations can provide a rationale or explanation for his or her behavior. In a similar fashion, the patient also needs to be given some rationale for how therapy is to be conducted and some explanation concerning the difficulties that have brought him or her to therapy. Humans do have a need to know what is happening to them, and a plausible explanation serves a therapeutic function. In the famous study of encounter groups conducted at Stanford University some years ago, those groups that were most successful emphasized the explanations and understanding secured (Lieberman, Yalom, & Miles, 1973). The recent growth of cognitive approaches to psychotherapy also lends some indirect support for the importance of cognitions and explanations in psychotherapy. The real issue, of course, is which explanations may be the most therapeutic.

As noted earlier, we have a bewildering number of schools of psychotherapy with their own theories and explanations about what factors have led to the patient's difficulties and what procedures are required for positive client change. Obviously, they can't all be right, and they differ tremendously. Thus, I and some others have hypothesized that some common factor must be at work here, and what is of therapeutic significance is the acceptance of the explanations by the client and not necessarily the scientific validity of these explanations (Frank, 1971; Garfield, 1980; van Kalmthout, Schaap, & Wojciechowski, 1985).

The interpretations and explanations offered by psychotherapists reflect the theoretical views and belief systems of the therapists. Clients being treated by psychoanalytically oriented therapists will be offered psychoanalytic insights and explanations. Clients receiving therapy from Adlerian therapists will be given explanations based on Adler's theoretical views—and so on for the various schools of psychotherapy. In each instance, the explanations are offered because they appear to the therapist to be appropriate within his or her own theoretical adherence and understanding. Apart from the issue of scientific validity, there are two aspects that are emphasized here. One is that the interpretations and explanations provided by a therapist who adheres closely to one specific theoretical orientation are necessarily limited. They cannot go beyond the confines of their theoretical orientation. The second point of emphasis, mentioned in the preceding paragraph, is that interpretations and explanations provided by the therapist must appear meaningful to the client and be accepted by the client. If not, it is doubtful that they will have any therapeutic value.

As compared with what can be called doctrinaire therapists (those that follow one theoretical orientation exclusively), eclectic psychotherapists have one possible advantage. Not being limited to one orientation, they can select interpretations or explanations from any theoretical persuasion that they believe fit the specific client being treated. If the facts of a given case appear to fit best with one theoretical explanation, the eclectic therapist is free to make use of it. However, as is the case with all psychotherapy, the explanation offered has to be accepted and eventually acted on by the client.

Emotional Release

Another potentially common feature occurring in many forms of psychotherapy is the opportunity for emotional release. In most approaches to psychotherapy, the client is allowed to discuss his or her problems, recount past and present events that have been upsetting, and express his or her feelings about such matters. The opportunity to unburden one's self about very troublesome guilt-inducing problems and related feelings may be quite therapeutic for some clients. Feelings or thoughts that could not be openly expressed or shared with others are more easily disclosed in the nonjudgmental and caring atmosphere characteristic of psychotherapy. The phenomenon of emotional catharsis or release has been noted and commented on during the entire history of psychotherapy. Although some forms of psychotherapy may emphasize the expression of feelings and emotions more than others, practically all of them provide an atmosphere that encourages or permits such expression. This is true even of behavioral forms of psychotherapy, as long as the therapist does not attempt to interfere with the expression of the client's feelings.

In a case that was being treated by a behavior therapist, the client, during one interview, began to relate highly emotionally charged material. Although in the previous sessions the focus was on learning relaxation procedures and developing an anxiety hierarchy, the client evidently had a need to express his feelings and share them with the therapist. The behavior therapist in this instance, to his credit, allowed the client to give free expression to his feelings and not insist on practicing the relaxation exercises. The client seemed to secure significant relief from this cathartic incident, and from that point on made speedy progress. The therapist regarded this incident as a critical factor in the therapy.

In the case of some patients with rather acute feelings of guilt, the expression of bottled-up affects can be quite marked and distinctly therapeutic. In other instances, emotional expression and release will be of lesser significance, but still be a functional part of the therapeutic process. Because this pattern of emotional release occurs across schools of psychotherapy and is of potential therapeutic value in a number of cases, it can be viewed as a common factor in psychotherapy.

Reinforcement

Another common factor in psychotherapy is the reinforcement provided by the therapist and the activities emanating from the therapeutic situation. Although most psychotherapists would probably state that they refrain from imposing their own values on the patient, there is little question that therapists do reinforce certain client behaviors. The behaviors, perceptions, and cognitions reinforced by the therapist, however, are related to the goals of therapy. Thus, therapists reinforce desired behaviors in a positive manner and use negative reinforcement or extinction procedures for undesirable behaviors. Although such

reinforcement patterns are most explicitly noted in programs emphasizing operant conditioning paradigms, they can also be observed in a
variety of other types of psychotherapy. Therapists convey approval
and encouragement by nodding their heads, smiling approvingly, and
offering a variety of verbal messages. For example, recorded cases seen
by Carl Rogers in client-centered therapy and analyzed by Truax (1966)
and Murray (1956) indicated that certain client responses were reinforced by positive reactions from Rogers. It seems clear, therefore, that
the therapist's responses do function in this manner and are of some
importance in affecting client change.

It would seem evident that psychotherapists, regardless of theoretical
orientation, make use of differential reinforcement. Nevertheless, it has
been mainly behavior therapists who have emphasized the importance
of reinforcement in therapy and who have been most explicit about its
use. However, to the extent that psychotherapy aims at changing the
client's maladaptive behavior, thoughts, and feelings, all therapists
should be aware of how such changes take place. Learning of some kind
would appear to be involved in this process, and reinforcement is an
important variable in facilitating learning.

In addition to the reinforcement offered by the therapist during the
actual therapy session, other activities that the therapist suggests the
patient engage in outside of therapy may also be reinforcing in a positive
manner. In some of the cognitive-behavior therapies, homework assignments are given to the patient to be carried out between sessions. The
patient may be encouraged to try out or practice some behaviors that he
or she may have tended to avoid previously and that play a role in his
or her difficulties. If these behaviors are performed successfully, they
also tend to be reinforced. In other instances, suggestions may be made
by the therapist in a less formal manner, and if followed up successfully
by the patient have a reinforcing effect on the behavior in question.

Consequently, reinforcement from the therapist is an important
feature of the therapeutic process and should be viewed as a factor
common to all forms of psychotherapy. Admittedly, it is stressed and
operationalized more by some forms of psychotherapy than by others.
However, it is an aspect of psychotherapy that is particularly important
in brief therapy. If the first few sessions go well and the patient believes
he or she is beginning to make progress, there is a greater probability of
a successful outcome (Garfield, 1986).

Desensitization

Another variable or process that appears to be operative in psychotherapy is that of desensitization. Although in more recent years the
behavioral procedure of systematic desensitization developed by Joseph

Wolpe (1958, 1961) has been the best known, there were earlier discussions of a less systematic process of desensitization (Garfield, 1957; Levine, 1948; Rosenzweig, 1936). The process referred to here pertains to the observation that as clients discuss their difficulties over a period of time in the therapy situation and share their problems with the therapist, the problems gradually appear to be less serious or troublesome. The repeated discussion with the therapist of matters that the client may have been preoccupied with and kept to him or herself appears to have a positive therapeutic effect. Unlike the process of catharsis, which is characterized by a strong release of emotion and affect at a particular time, the process of desensitization occurs over a period of time and is less dramatic.

By bringing troublesome issues out in the open, the client is able to discuss them with the therapist and to examine them in a more dispassionate manner. Thoughts and ideas that are shared with the therapist in this way also become less personalized and hence less threatening. As I noted in an earlier publication (Garfield, 1980):

> Personalized distortions and magnifications are more readily perceived and thus modified . . . with the help of the therapist. . . . In terms of a learning theory oriented explanation, the client's anxieties about these matters are gradually extinguished as he discusses them in the security of the therapeutic setting and no negative consequences are forthcoming. The fact that the therapist accepts the disclosures of the client without any evident show of surprise or concern may also contribute to this process of desensitization (p. 114).

This type of process would appear to occur in most forms of psychotherapy and to contribute to or facilitate progress in therapy. Not only are negative preoccupations or anxiety-provoking cognitions gradually perceived as less disturbing, but in discussing and revealing these matters in the therapy sessions the client may also become better able to face and resolve some of the factors responsible for his or her current state of discomfort.

Confronting One's Problems

All of us during our lifetime develop various procedures or defenses for overcoming or coping with the problems we encounter. One way of coping with anxiety-provoking or other types of noxious stimuli is to avoid them if at all possible. If an individual is very shy and feels extremely uncomfortable in social situations, he or she may attempt to avoid all such situations. Although such avoidance behavior does enable the individual to avoid or reduce feelings of discomfort, it has other undesirable effects. The individual misses out on the opportunities for social interaction and may feel quite inadequate and despondent as a result. However, as long as the individual continues avoidance behavior as the way to avoid social anxiety, there is little chance that his or her behavior will change for the better.

In order to help this type of individual, it is necessary to change the avoidance behavior into some type of approach behavior. Simply talking about the problem may not be sufficient to overcome it. However, if the client can be encouraged and supported to actually approach the situations he or she has avoided, there is an opportunity to secure some positive change. If the client enters the previously anxiety-avoiding situation and the expected negative consequences are not forthcoming, a reduction in the anxiety may ensue. This has a strong and positive effect on the client, and with repeated successful performance the client is able to change his or her social behavior to a significant degree.

Behavior therapists call this process exposure treatment. The use of exposure in vivo has been considered a particularly effective treatment for individuals suffering from agoraphobia (Emmelkamp, 1986; Mathews, Gelder, & Johnston, 1981). As such, it could be characterized as a specific treatment for agoraphobia rather than as a common variable in psychotherapy. However, helping a client confront his or her problems has a broader implication than just being exposed to the actual anxiety-provoking situation. There are also potential cognitive aspects, used by a variety of therapists, that essentially involve helping the client to face up to life situations realistically. Once this is accomplished, a number of specific actions can be suggested or recommended as a means of attaining the desired therapeutic goal. For example, such different procedures as systematic desensitization, implosion, or modeling have all been used to overcome specific avoidant behaviors. Furthermore, studies that have compared these different procedures have secured comparable results (Bandura, Blanchard, & Ritter, 1969; Erdwins, 1975; Gelder et al., 1973). What appears to be common in these approaches is that in all of them the client is confronted with the anxiety-inducing situation and discovers that there are no truly catastrophic conse-quences. Such indications of successful progress also increase the client's expectations of positive outcome and act as a reinforcement for the changed behavior.

There are other potential common factors that appear to be operative in most systems of psychotherapy. However, we do not discuss all such possible variables here. The purpose of this section is mainly to introduce some therapeutic variables that are not restricted to any one school of psychotherapy and that tend frequently to receive only limited emphasis or to be overlooked entirely. Yet, they appear to play an important part in the changes sought by psychotherapy. They are basic components of psychotherapy that should be understood and used intelligently by the psychotherapist.

In addition to common factors among the psychotherapies, there also are some factors or techniques that have been developed and used successfully for specific types of problems. Systematic desensitization, for example, is a treatment procedure developed by Wolpe (1958) for patients suffering with symptoms of anxiety. Exposure treatments, as previously noted, have been found particularly effective with cases of agoraphobia (Matthews et al., 1981). More recently, some degree of success has been reported with the combined use of both exposure and response prevention with obsessive-compulsive patients, a group that has been particularly difficult to treat (Emmelkamp, 1986). Similarly, a number of therapeutic approaches have been developed to treat such problems as bulimia (Weiss, Katzman, & Wolchik, 1985), lack of assertiveness and social skills deficits (Emmelkamp, 1986) and the like. Specific therapies of a brief type have also been developed for depression, but because there are a number of them and no clear superiority of one over the others, I am inclined to view them as primarily using some combination of common factors (Lewinsohn & Hoberman, 1982; Thompson, Gallagher, & Breckinbridge, 1987; Zeiss, Lewinsohn, & Munoz, 1979).

In essence, therefore, there appear to be a number of factors that are important in psychotherapy, and they certainly apply to brief psychotherapy. Some, designated as common therapeutic factors, are important in practically every case. Without a good therapeutic relationship, for example, it is difficult to see how positive results can be obtained regardless of the presenting problem. In a number of cases, the therapist usually will want also to use one or more special techniques or procedures in line with the specific problems of the patient. It is not an either/or proposition. The therapist who is not committed to following just one therapeutic approach thus has a number of options and procedures available. Some are part of the work with all patients, whereas some are selected for the specific patient. A wise selection and an appropriate application are deemed to provide the best results.

Chapter 3

Therapist Activities

The types of therapist activities and behaviors typical of brief therapy differ little from those that characterize longer-term psychotherapies, although their relative frequency of occurrence will differ. The expectancies concerning therapy and the therapist's stance will also differ. As noted in chapter 1, the therapist tends to be more active in brief therapy than in longer forms of therapy. However, if we analyze the activities of the brief therapist, we observe the same kinds of activities or behaviors as noted in most forms of psychotherapy. Although these may already be familiar to the reader, it is helpful to review them briefly. Too frequently in my own experience attention has been focused primarily on the hypothesized dynamics of the case and very little on the behaviors of the therapist. Consequently, we look at the therapeutic interactions in which the therapist is usually engaged.

LISTENING

Probably the most frequent activity of the therapist is that of listening. The therapist must be a good listener, and particularly in brief therapy must be attuned to what the patient is saying. Most of what the therapist learns about the patient comes from the information provided by the patient and from the therapist's observation of the patient during the therapy hour. Because what the patient relates has to be evaluated by the therapist, we can include the observation of the patient's behavior as a related aspect of listening. It is not only the verbal communication that conveys meaning but the manner in which it is delivered. Hesitations, anger, laughter, sarcasm, and related aspects of communication all are important in clarifying or elaborating on the spoken message. Although Theodore Reik's *Listening with the Third Ear* (1948) was written from a somewhat different perspective, the emphasis on a trained listener who is attuned to more than the spoken word is similar.

Listening on the part of the therapist (and also the client) is thus a basic component of psychotherapy, and the better the therapist is as a listener the more likely he or she is to understand the patient. Furthermore, the more the therapist understands the patient and his or her problems, the better the therapist can plan and conduct therapy. Listening and observing allow the therapist to evaluate the information provided by the client. If any material is unclear or there appear to be significant gaps in what the client relates, the therapist must respond in a meaningful manner, e.g. ask for elaboration and clarification as judged appropriate or, if it appears the client has some reasons for omitting potentially important material, to hold off for a while. However, decisions need to be made quickly, for one cannot delay very long when conducting brief psychotherapy.

Listening in brief therapy is thus an active process and is linked to other processes or activities. While listening, the therapist evaluates the client's utterances, observes his or her behavior, decides whether to question the client or delay such questions, offers comments, interpretations, and suggestions, and may even change the focus of the interaction. The therapist should also be particularly attentive to any comments about the therapy or the therapist, regardless of how fleetingly stated, because these bear on the client's view of therapy and need to be carefully explored.

Listening, therefore, is far from a simple activity and requires considerable practice. The best exercise I know is to go over taped sessions, with a supervisor preferably at times, and note the number of times you should have made a response and did not or the times you verbalized when it cut off the client's flow of significant material, or when your comments did not really respond to what the client was saying. Frequently, in my own supervisory experience when listening to taped sessions, students exclaim in surprise: "How could I have missed that?" or "I don't know why I said that." Such comments indicate that listening, to be effective, must be closely linked with attention and evaluation. The therapist constantly has to evaluate what is going on in order to respond in the most appropriate or therapeutic manner.

REFLECTION

Another category of therapist response that has been particularly studied and emphasized by client-centered therapists is reflection. This refers to the therapist's ability to reflect the attitudes of the client in an empathic manner (Rogers, 1951). It is also closely tied to listening, because accurate and sensitive reflections depend on the client being understood by the therapist.

The process or activity of reflection is important in psychotherapy for several reasons. It conveys to the patient that the therapist is both listening and trying to understand the nature of his or her difficulties. Such behavior also indicates the therapist's interest in trying to help the patient. It may be a significant means of communicating empathy with the patient and his or her situation. It may also be a reinforcing variable that encourages the patient to disclose personal and discomforting thoughts and feelings to the therapist. To the extent that the therapist reflects the patient's attitudes and feelings accurately and sensitively, he or she shows sincere interest in the patient and helps to create a positive therapeutic relationship—the foundation for future therapeutic work.

Although the reflection of attitudes and feelings may seem to be a fairly straightforward activity on the part of the therapist, it should not be regarded in an overly simplistic manner. How the reflection is verbalized is exceedingly important, because it can be interpreted by the patient in different ways. For example, a therapist, after listening to a patient offer a number of self-criticisms, says "So, you really can't do anything right." Both the words chosen and the tone of speaking could be interpreted by the patient as criticism and disapproval, an interaction that usually would not contribute to a good therapeutic relationship. In contrast, a reflection phrased as follows might be received quite differently: "So, whatever you try doesn't seem to work out too well." Stated in a sincere manner by the therapist, this reflection conveys understanding and empathy, which may encourage the patient to continue to reveal the feelings that are sources of discomfort. Such a response also contributes to the development of a positive patient-therapist relationship.

Reflection, consequently, is a manifestation of the empathic response or the ability of the therapist to fully resonate to the feelings expressed by the client and to communicate this to the client. Rogers (1951), in emphasizing the importance of the counselor's empathic response in the counseling process, offered the following formulation:

> This formulation would state that it is the counselor's function to assume, in so far as he is able, the internal frame of reference of the client, to perceive the world as the client sees it, to perceive the client himself as he is seen by himself, to lay aside all perceptions from the external frame of reference while doing so, and to communicate something of this empathic understanding to the client. (p. 29)

Reflection has sometimes been referred to as the sensitivity of the clinician. The good therapist must be sensitive to what the patient is trying to communicate about his or her problems, feelings, and attitudes. If the therapist does not understand fully what the patient is communicating or trying to communicate, the chances for effective treatment are lessened. However, empathy or the empathic response is more than this. It also includes the message from the therapist that the patient is fully understood—not just the verbal communication, but also the feelings associated with it. The empathic response, consequently, facilitates the development of a therapeutic alliance between therapist and patient and increases the probability of a positive outcome. To the extent that the patient feels understood by the therapist, he or she no longer experiences being alone, and there is increased hope that change is possible.

Reflections thus are a regular aspect of the psychotherapeutic interaction but should not be carried out in a perfunctory or overly repetitive fashion. Rather, they should be used naturally and with sincerity. They are particularly important in the early sessions, because they play a role in the impressions the client forms about the therapist and therapy.

SUGGESTION

From time to time in psychotherapy, it is not unusual for the therapist to offer some suggestions to the client. Suggestions have been viewed in the past as rather directive therapist behaviors and have been looked down on by both dynamically oriented and client-centered therapists. In more recent times, suggestions have tended to be superceded by more explicit homework assignments on the part of cognitive and behavioral therapists. Nevertheless, as noted in the previous chapter, even well-known behavior therapists make use of suggestion, and this is undoubtedly true of other therapists as well.

There is really nothing wrong with offering suggestions to clients if they are sought in a meaningful way and offer some possibility of helping the client. In some instances, it makes sense to suggest to the client several different ways of attempting to handle a problem. This is certainly true when there is no obvious or preferred solution. Also, there may be potentially less feelings of guilt or inadequacy if suggestions are not carried out as compared to when explicit homework assignments are not completed.

Suggestions can be made in very different ways. Some suggestions can be made in ways that resemble directives or military orders. Others can be made in a more open-ended fashion, for example, "Do you think that setting a schedule for your household activities might be a good idea?" By offering a suggestion in this manner, the therapist is more likely to get the client's response to the suggestion and some discussion about it. It may be that the client's response may lead to a modification of the suggestion or to the selection of a better alternative. Such a process fosters more of a client-therapist collaboration than if the suggestions were "handed down from on high."

In the absence of any systematically acquired research data on the therapeutic importance of suggestions, it is difficult to make any truly adequate appraisal of their value in brief psychotherapy. Furthermore, one should also distinguish between suggestions that seem helpful to the patient and move therapy forward and suggestions that may have a more negative effect. As is true with all procedures and techniques in psychotherapy, judgment and skill are required for positive application. If, for example, I were treating a patient who complained that his wife or his mother were always telling him what to do, I'd be rather cautious in offering a number of suggestions. The individual patient and the existing therapeutic relationship have to be taken into account. Some patients are more suggestible and cooperative, some seek suggestions, and some are quite resistant.

Suggestions, in my view, have a place in brief psychotherapy. They appear to have been used as a therapeutic procedure for some time and can be observed in the ongoing psychotherapy interactions today. The therapist can use them most advantageously in a cooperative way in which the patient also participates by helping to evaluate the suggestions made.

EXPLANATION AND INTERPRETATION

We have already discussed the role of explanations and interpretations in psychotherapy and thus can be quite brief here. As already noted, psychotherapists frequently offer explanations and interpretations. Clients are frequently mystified by their own behavior, thoughts, or feelings, and seek some explanation from their therapists. Consequently, providing explanations seems a natural part of the therapeutic process.

Other related aspects pertain to the fact that the human being relies a great deal on verbal activities, thinking or cognitive activity, and on learning. Different approaches to psychotherapy may emphasize certain aspects more than others, but all involve explanations or interpretations to some extent. The explanations offered by the therapist not only may help assuage certain anxieties the patient has about his or her problems, but they also indicate the therapist's understanding of these problems. If the explanations are received positively by the patient, they help to strengthen the therapeutic relationship and the patient's positive view of the therapist. On the other hand, if the explanations or interpretations are perceived by the patient as farfetched or as critical, they would more likely have a negative effect. Thus, how the explanation is offered and the quality of the patient-therapist relationship may be as important as the explanation itself.

As is true of other therapist interventions, therefore, the therapist must assess the client and the progress of the therapy when offering an interpretation or explanation. Explanations should not be offered in a dogmatic or accusing manner. Rather, they can be mentioned in a manner that essentially asks the client about his or her response or evaluation of the explanation. Such prefixes as "It seems likely" tend to lessen the dogmatic quality of an interpretation. These statements can also be followed by such questions as "What do you think?" or "Does that make sense to you?"

In addition to offering the client possible explanations about his or her difficulties where appropriate, the therapist also provides the client with some explanation or rationale about the treatment. It is important to do so for several reasons. The client may enter therapy with expectations that are unrealistic or incongruent with the type of therapy to be conducted. It is desirable, therefore, to orient the client to what will be taking place and why. The client can also be informed of his or her role in therapy and the importance of cooperation and compliance. Thus, both therapist and client can start with similar expectations about what will be taking place in therapy.

PROVIDING INFORMATION

In the preceding section, the role of the therapist in offering interpretations and explanations to the client was discussed. Such activities potentially cover a wide range of therapist inputs and are influenced to a large extent by the theoretical orientation of the therapist. The therapist, however, is not limited to such verbal interactions. He or she may also provide information that is more akin to scientific or general knowledge and that is not based on an analysis of the client's behavior as it relates to a specific theory. Although providing information and offering interpretations and explanations may appear similar or overlapping, they are not really identical. In fact, whereas dynamic therapists have emphasized the importance of accurate interpretations of repressed material and defenses, they have not been equally positive about information. Providing information to the client has been viewed primarily as an intellectual activity placing the therapist in an overly directive role. Such a pattern was viewed as interfering with the active role of the client in trying to recover repressed affects and conflicts.

It is true that if therapy becomes structured in such a manner that the patient asks questions and the therapist answers them, the therapy session becomes a question-and-answer period, and other types of explanation and learning will be diminished. However, there is a legitimate place in psychotherapy for providing patients with relevant information. Some patients have information deficits or distortions that contribute to their difficulties. Consequently, when the correct information is provided, some positive change can occur.

A number of illustrations can be given concerning the potential usefulness of correct information. For example, at present a large number of people are anxious about possibly contracting AIDS. Some of them may actually have phobias about this that require more specific and directed treatment. Others, however, can be helped considerably by simply being informed as to how the disease is actually transmitted.

Some individuals may have inaccurate or distorted conceptions of their own psychological difficulties. They may interpret some signs of anxiety or compulsive behavior as an indication that they are "going crazy." A calmly presented bit of information concerning the frequent incidence of such symptoms and the fact that they in no way indicate that the individual is about to become psychotic is both informative and reassuring. In my own experience, a few persons who had feelings of guilt about such matters as masturbation or hostility toward their parents were helped by seeing some of their behavior as not unusual or atypical.

Providing accurate information to the client about important personal matters thus may be a worthwhile activity. This does not mean that therapy emphasizes providing information. It is just one of the many kinds of activities that may be used judiciously when appropriate for the problem at hand. Obviously, the information must be relevant to the problem and the goals of therapy. If the client asks for information that is not relevant, such questions have to be handled differently. Questions about the weather, the local baseball team, TV programs, movies, and the like in most instances are not directly relevant, and the therapist has to decide why they are being asked and respond appropriately. Personal questions about the therapist also have to be evaluated. Do they reflect concern about the therapist's competence? Do they convey the feeling that the client wants to make the relationship more of a social one? and so forth.

As is true of most of the therapist's interventions, the frequency of giving information to the client will vary with the client. Clients obviously differ in their overall knowledge and in terms of information deficits. The therapist, throughout therapy, must evaluate what is taking place, both in terms of what the client is saying and doing and in terms of what interventions would be most helpful. If the therapist finds him or herself delivering long segments of information that tend to resemble lectures, then he or she may be overusing this procedure to the possible detriment of the therapeutic process.

CONFRONTATION

Another type of therapist behavior is confrontation. Although confrontation carries a rather negative connotation, it does have a place in psychotherapy and, as with all psychotherapeutic procedures, must be used wisely and appropriately. Confrontation, in particular, is a procedure that can have negative consequences when misused.

Although confrontation has been employed in varying ways by therapists with different orientations, its general objective is to challenge the patient in some way. Because patients tend to be troubled people and generally have low self-esteem, confronting them about some personal deficiency is not a matter to be taken lightly. After all, therapy, hopefully, should help people and not add to their troubles. Consequently, the therapist must be particularly sensitive and adroit concerning the use of confrontation. First of all, a good therapeutic relationship needs to have been established, with the patient having confidence in the therapist's desire to help him or her. If this is lacking, the patient may view the confrontation as an attack, may become upset, and may leave therapy. Second, the therapist needs to confront the patient in a manner that conveys the therapist's interest in aiding the patient—and this in no way is a double-binded message. This is the way that many good parents interact with their children and still convey their parental love. One can question certain behaviors without really impairing a relationship.

Having emphasized the importance of how confrontations are handled in psychotherapy, we discuss the kinds of situations where they may be used. In most situations where there appears to be an important contradiction or inconsistency in what the patient relates, I believe the patient should be confronted, even in a relatively early session. For example, if the patient says she gets along very well with everyone but also mentions difficulties with several people, she could be confronted with this discrepancy and some clarification could be attempted. This might lead to a better understanding of the patient's actual difficulties with others. I once worked with a man who complained that all of the people he did business with took advantage of him. I confronted him with the fact that he sought these people out and literally asked them to take advantage of him. In this case, confrontation was deemed appropriate because the patient had avoided facing the implications of his own behavior as a recurring cause of his difficulties. When he was able to recognize and accept the reality of what was occurring, he was able to go through the process of attempting to change his behavior.

Inexperienced therapists sometimes appear very reluctant or unable to confront their clients when some type of confrontation appears necessary. In some instances, this seemingly reflects a lack of assertiveness on the part of the therapist. Therapists, after all, differ in personality. In other instances, therapists convey the impression that they always have to be kind and friendly. Thus, confrontation is perceived as a rather negative and unkind intervention. Although confrontation can be nontherapeutic, as noted earlier, it is an overgeneralization to say it is always so. Clearly, there are times when individuals need to be confronted with patterns of behavior that are self defeating, and this process will facilitate progress in therapy. Conversely, avoidance of such intervention may prolong therapy unnecessarily.

Because confrontation may be viewed less positively than the other therapist behaviors, some additional elaboration and examples are worth presenting. There are some nonglamorous aspects of psychotherapy that often call for confrontation on the part of the therapist: for example, the client being late for the therapy session, missing therapy sessions, and failing to pay the therapist's fees. When a patient exhibits such patterns, it is important that he or she be confronted about these patterns. There are also a number of other instances where it is clinically important to confront the patient about his or her participation in therapy. I recall seeing a client who verbalized in a nonstop fashion and actually seemed to say very little. Because she was prompt and conscientious about her appointments and otherwise seemed interested in therapy, I listened, nodded my head, said, 'hmm hmm," reflected her feelings, and avoided any type of confrontation. I expected that my empathic style would gradually produce a change in the client's behavior and more meaningful material would emerge. I was wrong, for the same pattern continued and I felt no real progress was made. As a result, I decided to confront her with what I regarded as evasive behavior. This produced a strong response. My confrontation apparently allowed her to discuss her feelings about me and her negative views of the therapy. I regarded this as important, even though I would have preferred a more positive response. It led to her decision to terminate therapy, with which I concurred. Although not a successful outcome, in my judgment it was better to have resolved the matter relatively early than later, and preferable to having the client withdraw from therapy without having a chance to express and discuss her feelings.

Having provided an example with a negative outcome, let me add one other outcome of confrontation that was more positive. During an initial interview with a young woman, I asked her to tell me about what things were bothering her and what she hoped could be accomplished in therapy. She was very forthright and forceful in her manner and mentioned several things that she hoped she could be helped with in therapy. As she talked, I was favorably impressed with how well organized she was and with the reasonableness of her expectations. Then, very unexpectedly, after thinking for a few seconds, she stated that she would like to become more self-assertive. This was the last thing I would have expected to hear from this rather assertive woman, and almost intuitively I said "You want to become *more* assertive?" Again, she thought for a few moments, and then said, "I see what you mean. I guess not." In this instance, time apparently was saved by my response. I also thought that my confrontation communicated that I was attentive to what she said and also that I knew what was realistic in terms of therapy. In any event, this case progressed very well and very quickly.

Finally, I add a note of caution. Confrontation has its utility and proper place in psychotherapy. It also can have a more negative impact on the client than many of the other behaviors discussed, although interpretations and explanations can also have such an impact depending on what they are and how they are delivered. Consequently, the therapist needs to evaluate very carefully the effect a confrontation has on a client and judge the effect of possible future confrontations accordingly. Also, if confrontations become frequent and lead to disputations, the therapist should view this as a serious problem and think of ways to resolve it. It may be symptomatic of an undesirable therapeutic relationship.

REASSURANCE

Another therapist activity is reassurance. Although not always accorded a role of importance, particularly among psychodynamic theorists, reassurance from the psychotherapist may be a worthwhile therapeutic intervention. It has been viewed as a supportive technique, but there is really nothing wrong with supportive techniques when used intelligently. Reassurance, when overused or used without adequate justification, will generally have little positive impact. There are, however, instances when reassurance can be part of a positive therapeutic interaction. Reassurance can also be used quite naturally when certain information is provided to the patient.

Most psychotherapists will at some time encounter patients with either vague or specific concerns about their particular symptoms or behavior. Reassurance concerning the probabilities of being helped or even that the symptoms in question are by no means unusual can be quite comforting to the patient. Where patients overreact with anxiety about some incident or occurrence, in part because of misinformation, the correct information accompanied by reassurance can be quite therapeutic.

It is clear, however, that the reassuring statements of the therapist must be borne out by the actual life experiences of the client. If they are, then they also function as a positive reinforcement. On the other hand, if the therapist reassures the client that his or her symptoms will disappear within a specified period of time, and in fact they do not, then it is likely that the effect will be negative. In the latter instance, false expectations have been generated, and when they are not fulfilled the client may be worse off than before. Thus, reassurance should be given selectively in those instances where the therapist is confident of the situation. Those of us who have had a growth or tumor and have been told after a biopsy that it is not malignant know how reassuring this statement is. However, such feelings would be of course change drastically if the statement were later proven false. Although the situations in psychotherapy may not be as dramatic, false or inappropriate reassurance can have a negative effect. It depends on how the reassurance is given and the nature of the matter discussed.

HOMEWORK ASSIGNMENTS

Assignments made by the therapist to be completed outside of the therapy session have been emphasized mainly by cognitive and behavioral therapists. However, their potential utility in psychotherapy generally has become increasingly recognized. Such assignments can be used with a variety of problems, as discussed shortly. What should be emphasized is that carrying out assignments essentially involves a process of learning. Thus, the task should be one that the client has a reasonable chance of mastering and for which the client is sufficiently motivated. As we know, "nothing succeeds like success," and the therapist must evaluate homework assignments accordingly.

Homework assignments have been used successfully in cases of social anxiety or shyness, in cases of agoraphobia, in depression, in cases with sexual difficulties, in work with marital problems, and in both individual and group psychotherapy. The type of assignments have varied and apparently are limited only by the ingenuity of the therapist. In some instances (for example, in cases dealing with bulimia), diaries or daily records may be kept. In these instances, the client will note the individual food items consumed, the time, the setting, and any related incidents or feelings. In the case of agoraphobia, the client, in cooperation with a spouse or significant other, may venture out with specified objectives or goals.

The use of homework assignments and practice in the area of sexual therapy has been popularized by the work of Masters and Johnson (1970) and needs no additional mention here. Marital therapy is another area that lends itself well to the use of homework assignments. Various kinds of communication exercises can be assigned depending on the problems manifested by particular couples. In addition, records can be kept during the week of specific kinds of interactions, activities, and the like. Also, because most marital therapy is conducted with couples, there would appear to be a greater chance for the homework assignments to be completed or the true story of lack of compliance to be reported at the next session of therapy.

The therapist must decide what assignments may be useful and what amount is reasonable. As with some of the other components of therapy, it is a good procedure to discuss the assignment with the client and to get his or her opinion about it. Although it is the therapist's responsibility to direct therapy, a collaboration of therapist and client generally facilitates progress.

One of the reasons that homework assignments have come to play a more important role in psychotherapy is that they are related to real-life activities that occur outside of the therapist's office. As a result, the possible generalization effects of any changes obtained are greater than might otherwise be obtained. They also help to demonstrate to the client that meaningful changes are possible and that psychotherapy is more than just talk.

The preceding statements obviously are predicated on successful uses of homework assignments. As is true with other features of psychotherapy, the use of homework assignments does not always lead to the desired results. In such instances, the therapist must evaluate the possible reasons for the limited outcome. Was the assignment premature or too difficult? Did the client make only a halfhearted attempt to follow through on the assignment? In the case of a couple, is one partner subtly sabotaging the work at home? What is the client's perception of the situation? There are clearly a number of possibilities that may be considered in evaluating a particular case.

The issue of not completing assignments, or noncompliance, is another aspect that needs careful appraisal by the therapist. In such cases, the patient would generally be viewed as resisting the therapeutic efforts of the therapist. The therapist not only must query the patient about this but also must appraise the reasons given by the patient. In some instances, this may involve a confrontation with the patient concerning the patient's obvious lack of cooperation. In other instances, depending on the stage of therapy and the patient's previous behavior, it may be wise to simply query the patient and see if the patient will try to carry out the assignment in the coming week. In one case that I worked with, I appeared to have a textbook case of psychologically determined forgetting. Among other things, the patient was keeping a diary of food intake and was to bring it to our session. For four successive weeks she forgot to bring the diary. The weight problem was not really the patient's main reason for seeking therapy, but it was a concrete problem that I thought we could include in our early work in therapy. For this reason, I did not really confront her about forgetting to bring the diary. After these four sessions, the patient brought up the critical problem that she felt she could now share with me. From that point on, therapy went very well and at a quick pace. When we terminated 2 months later, she told me voluntarily that she had lost 10 pounds on her own.

How assignments are used and with what frequency undoubtedly will be determined according to the therapist's preferences and the nature of the individual case. In some instances, the therapist may offer suggestions instead of making more formal homework assignments. In either case, the therapist is encouraging the client to engage in extratherapy behaviors that are related to the goals of therapy and will facilitate progress toward those goals.

MODELING AND ROLE PLAYING

Another activity that is used by psychotherapists is role playing. This, also, can be used in a variety of ways. It can be used to have the client act out something that has happened in the past, or it can be used in helping the client practice behaviors for an anticipated future event. The emphasis here is on actual behavior or performance instead of just verbal speech or utterances.

In role playing, the therapist may or may not play a part. In individual therapy, it is more likely that the therapist will be an active participant taking on one of the roles. In marital or couples therapy, the role playing is more likely to be done by the clients with the therapist functioning in the role of director.

Although role playing is not advocated and used by psychoanalytically oriented therapists, it has been used in different ways by therapists for a number of years. Recently, role playing has been used by behavioral and cognitive therapists, and some have referred to it as behavioral rehearsal. Whatever the name, it is a potentially useful technique and can be adapted to the particular needs of a given patient.

For helping patients with problems of assertiveness and other social skills, the use of role plays is quite helpful. For example, if a person feels he lacks the confidence to assert himself in relationship to his supervisor, this situation can be set up with the therapist playing the role of the supervisor. The client can then go through the actual behavior of making an assertion, asking for a raise, or the like. Furthermore, if the client's behavior is far from the desired goal, the roles can be reversed and the therapist can play the role of the patient. There are, of course, limits to the roles that can be reenacted in therapy—at least in individual therapy. For example, if the client's lack of assertiveness or social skills involves a member of the opposite sex, I must admit that I do not function well in that type of role. In such instances, other procedures, perhaps homework assignments, may be more efficacious.

The therapist can function as a model in at least two ways. As already mentioned, he or she can model specific behaviors that the client needs to master in order to function more effectively. In a more general and inclusive sense, the therapist may also serve as a model for the client in terms of his or her interactions with the client throughout therapy. To the extent that the therapist is viewed positively by the client, the client may tend to model some of the behaviors and values of the therapist. The results of a few studies have indicated some convergence in the beliefs of therapists and clients at the conclusion of therapy and their relationship to outcome (Beutler, Crago, & Arizmendi, 1986). Although one should not overgeneralize from such results, it does lend at least a bit of support to the potential influence of the therapist as a model for the client.

QUESTIONING

Because therapists do ask questions of the client, it is worth paying some attention to this therapist behavior. Generally, the therapist may ask more questions in the initial sessions than later on, because he or she is interested in securing basic information about the client. This is a natural component of the beginning phase of therapy, and we discuss it further in the next chapter. As therapy proceeds, the number of questions may decrease, but there will always be occasions to ask questions of the client.

As a general rule, the therapist needs to ask questions when there is inadequate information about any topic of importance. This may relate to such matters as the duration of the client's problems, possible precipitating events, previous treatment, how the client felt during the past week, if assignments were completed, what made the client late for the therapy session, and when the therapist's fee will be paid. Questions can cover a wide range of items. As with all aspects of therapy, the therapist should have some rationale for his or her questions and be prepared to follow up as necessary.

Among the things the therapist should keep in mind is the possible effect of his or her questions. The therapist can ask very direct questions in the style of a legal interrogator or interviewer. Such a pattern is more likely to accentuate factual matters over feelings and possibly to lead to a question-and-answer style of interaction. It also overemphasizes the role of the therapist at the expense of a more collaborative relationship. Thus, although the relationship should definitely be a professional rather than a "folksy" one, it need not be so rigidly structured. The therapist can ask questions in a way that allows the client to relate information in a more natural manner, for example, "Perhaps you can tell me what went on at the time and how you felt about it" is preferable to "What happened?" "How did you feel?"

There are two final points to mention. If the client relates something that is not clear and it is of some importance, the therapist should try to clarify the matter unless there is some reason not to do so. I have noted many times that student therapists have said, "hmm, hmm" or "I see" in response to a client statement, but when questioned really did not know what the client meant. It is much better to say "I don't understand" when you really don't understand than to say "I see."

Finally, in contrast to prosecuting attorneys, the therapist usually is not interested in a yes or no answer. Such answers usually require another question or similar response from the therapist. "What were your feelings when that happened" will generally bring forth a more descriptive and meaningful response than "Were you upset when that happened?"

SELF-DISCLOSURE

Relating some personal incident or experience to the patient occurs in therapy and has actually been emphasized by some approaches to psychotherapy (Jourard, 1971). Self-disclosure also has more than one meaning (Ivey & Authier, 1978), but here I refer only to the therapist recounting a personal experience.

Based on my own experience, I believe that an occasional self-disclosure, when it appears germane to the patient's problem, may have some positive impact on the patient. This statement should be viewed cautiously, because I have no real data to support it. However, I present my views.

The points to be emphasized first are the occasional use of self-disclosure and the relevance of the self-disclosure for the patient's problem. I would be quite concerned if the therapist's self-disclosures were frequent and seemed to be more a function of the therapist's needs than of their relevance for the patient's therapy. However, if such self-disclosures occur only infrequently and seem to arise naturally out of the ongoing interaction in therapy, they may be potentially positive.

Such self-disclosure may, first of all, reflect the interest of the therapist in the client, because the client's experience strikes a responsive chord in the therapist. They also indicate that the therapist is a real person and has had some experience that is comparable to that which the patient has experienced. This resembles an empathic response. In addition, the therapist, in recounting personal experience, may also be modeling a means of coping with a problem. Patients appear to pay particular interest to such occasional disclosures and to remember them. At the same time, overly personal items are best avoided, and the therapist's personal problems should not be shared with the patient.

SUMMARY OF THERAPIST ACTIVITIES

A variety of therapist activities and operations have been described in this chapter. Although they may not include all possible activities of the therapist, they do include those that are most prominent and most frequent. They also represent activities or procedures that are not limited to one particular theoretical orientation. For purposes of exposition, most of these therapist activities were described individually. However, it should be apparent that these activities overlap and interact as the therapist is conducting therapy.

The therapist clearly is engaged very actively in the process of brief psychotherapy. Most of the activities described entail an active stance on the part of the therapist. Even listening to the client is an active process, because the therapist is at the same time observing the client, evaluating what is being said, and formulating an appropriate response or intervention. The therapist also communicates by means of bodily gestures, facial expressions, smiling, nodding, and the like. Consequently, he or she must be aware not only of what the client is saying and doing, but also of what kinds of impressions he or she is making on the client. This process of psychotherapeutic activity essentially constitutes the rest of this book.

Chapter 4

The Initial Interview

The initial interview is without question exceedingly important, and a number of considerations must be kept in mind. The therapist will be interested in evaluating the patient in terms of a number of criteria. What type of problem or problems are presented by the patient? How serious are these problems? How interested or motivated is the patient in collaborating with the therapist in the necessary therapeutic work? What potential strengths and weaknesses does the patient seem to have? Are there particular stresses or crises in the patient's life that complicate the situation? Is brief therapy a suitable procedure for this patient, and what are the chances for a truly positive outcome? Finally, the therapist should evaluate also his or her personal reaction to the patient and the prospect for a favorable therapeutic relationship.

It is evident, therefore, that the therapist needs to consider a number of different items pertaining to the patient and to the future therapeutic interactions. The therapist needs to be especially alert and active to secure and evaluate the necessary information in a relatively short time. In essence, the goal is a rapid but adequate assessment.

The assessment of the client can mean different things to clinicians, depending on their training and orientation. To some this may mean a long and detailed life history assessment with an emphasis on early development. To others, assessment may signify the use of a battery of psychological tests. Behavior therapists have emphasized a behavioral assessment, although some of them have also begun to utilize tests and rating scales (Swann & MacDonald, 1978). For purposes of research or recordkeeping it is useful to employ some systematic or standard assessment procedure that is used with every client. However, I do not believe that such a procedure is necessary in the daily practice of brief psychotherapy, particularly if the assessment procedure is lengthy or adds to the client's cost of treatment. On the other hand, the use of a brief self-rating scale for the client and also one for the therapist may be a feasible procedure.

Based on my own experience, I have taken a rather critical view concerning the use of psychometric instruments with reference to psychotherapy. I believe strongly that whatever is done in therapy or clinical work generally should be done for the patient's benefit. Extensive assessment of the patient must be adequately justified, because it may entail extra cost and may delay the initiation of therapy. Consequently, routine testing does not appear required unless it will facilitate the therapeutic process or shorten the time required for psychotherapy. I do not know of any body of systematic research that has clearly provided support for such use. Thus, the therapist, in his or her initial interview with the patient, must decide, among other things, whether or not additional or specialized assessment is desirable. In a clinical setting where a different intake worker has provided an initial impression of the patient, the therapist has some preliminary information on which to base any clinical inquiries he wants to make for client assessment. In settings where the therapist makes the first contact with the patient, the therapist obviously relies primarily on personal observation and appraisal.

In most cases, the therapist will be able to secure the information and make the evaluations that are necessary during the first interview. We have already mentioned the kinds of considerations that are of importance during this interview. If there are no indications of severe pathology or no questions about the patient's level of integration, the focus generally will be on the patient's complaints or problems, his or her suitability for treatment, and on some decision concerning acceptance for therapy. However, if the diagnostic appraisal is unclear or there is some concern about the degree of pathology, then additional assessment, consultation, or referral needs to be considered. At this point, the therapist may decide on the use of psychological tests (administered by the therapist or by others) to clarify the diagnostic problem. The therapist may also decide to have the patient examined by a neurologist or refer the patient for treatment to someone else.

In cases where there is some question about the integration or pathology of the client, a decision to undertake psychotherapy is postponed and the final decision may turn out to be a negative one. Where such concerns are not involved, the focus is on matters pertaining more directly to psychotherapy.

THE PATIENT'S STRENGTHS, WEAKNESSES, AND PERSONAL STYLE

In evaluating a patient for brief psychotherapy, the therapist tries initially to see if the problem or problems presented by the client are appropriate for this form of therapy. As indicated, acute psychotic disorders and severe personality disorders are not prime candidates for this type of treatment. Mild to moderate cases of anxiety disorders and depression can respond successfully with varying degrees of success depending on how the therapy is conducted. Severe depression is more problematic and may require consultation and medication. As a result, the therapist will make some diagnostic appraisal during the initial session to determine the client's suitability. In doing so, he or she will generally ask for a description of what is bothering the client, the duration of the problem, possible precipitating circumstances, previous treatment, and any related questions that arise from the discussion. As indicated, this need not be a lengthy or detailed inquiry unless the diagnostic picture is not clear. In this instance, an additional interview may be required before a decision is reached. In most cases, however, this will not be necessary, and the therapist will be concerned with evaluating other aspects of the individual.

The patient's personality and style of interacting with the therapist also constitute a major item for appraisal during the initial interview, with several different implications. For example, whether the patient appears bright or slow, is energetic or phlegmatic, blames others or self, or is demanding or beseeching—are all features that need to be evaluated in terms of how the patient will function in therapy and what kind of difficulties might be anticipated. The patient's ability to express his or her feelings or to discuss personal matters of concern are also of importance. Is it easy to get the required information, or is it "like pulling teeth"? Does the patient over-dramatize incidents, or are important matters pushed aside?

Patients differ in many respects, and they have patterns of strengths and weaknesses, assets and deficiencies. Therapists, for the most part, have preferences concerning desirable patients. They seem to prefer patients who are likeable, not too disturbed, intelligent, and interested in psychotherapy. In a study of the ratings of 13 psychotherapists (Garfield & Affleck, 1961), it was concluded that "On the basis of such ratings, one might infer that the average therapist prefers a patient who is intelligent, anxious, well motivated for therapy, young, and with some insight into his difficulties!" (p. 507). Clearly, therapists welcome bright, articulate, pleasant, and motivated patients, and this is easily understood. They are nice people to work with, and the results are generally positive. Unfortunately, not all individuals who have problems and seek help possess all of these desirable characteristics. Nevertheless, these less fortunate or less well-endowed persons also need to be helped.

Although therapists appear to prefer intelligent patients, the available research literature does not indicate any particular intellectual level as a necessary cutoff point for psychotherapy (Garfield, 1986). Also, not all individuals with IQs over 135 are necessarily the most desirable cases or secure the most positive outcomes. Other personal qualities are clearly important. Thus, one finds frequent references to the importance of the patient's motivation. A willing and able collaborator in therapy is evaluated positively. A resistant, rigid, and hostile individual, on the other hand, is regarded more negatively and presents more potential difficulties in terms of the therapeutic relationship. A very passive and dependent individual also may present particular difficulties in therapy, but of a different sort, and of course must be handled differently.

Other items that may also be important concerning possible strengths and weaknesses in the patient pertain to the patient's life situation, work record, and social support system. These obviously interact with and influence the patient's adjustment and prognosis. An unhappy marital situation, a difficulty in securing adequate employment, and excessive demands placed on the individual by others all tend to be factors that make the therapeutic task more difficult.

All of the items just described convey information to the therapist about the patient and how he or she responds in the interview, and all have implications for future patient-therapist interactions. Although the therapist's initial appraisal of the patient may be modified as therapy proceeds, the initial impressions form the basis for the therapist's decision concerning the acceptance of the patient for brief therapy. These impressions are also influential in the general expectations that the therapist develops about how therapy will proceed and about potential problems that may surface later.

As noted, there are three overlapping but distinct features of the client that the therapist needs to attend to and evaluate. One concerns the client's clinical problem and degree of psychopathology, particularly with reference to the patient's ability to benefit from brief psychotherapy. A second concerns the client's personal qualities and style of relating to others. The third feature, which may overlap either of the first two, or both, essentially refers to the personal impression the client makes on the therapist. In other words, how does the therapist, personally, respond to the client as an individual? Although this latter consideration is not always given much attention in practice, it is an aspect of psychotherapy that deserves some attention. Psychoanalytically oriented therapists have referred to the term countertransference when discussing overly strong feelings the therapist has toward the patient during therapy. I do not believe it is necessary to use this term, with its excessive conceptual baggage. However, it is important that the therapist be aware of whatever feelings he or she may have toward the patient. Such feelings should be evaluated as objectively as possible during the initial interview. If the therapist has any personal qualms about accepting the patient for therapy, it is probably best not to accept the individual and to refer him or her elsewhere or have an additional interview before reaching a final decision.

Some examples can be used to illustrate the preceding statements. I recall several instances where interns or relatively inexperienced therapists were very much afraid of the cases assigned to them. In one instance, a male psychology intern told me he was afraid of being assaulted by the patient assigned to him by his supervisor. He described the patient as a large and potentially dangerous young man. Because of the intern's concerns, I agreed to see the patient myself. Much to my surprise, the patient was a small, swaggering adolescent whom I could not see as dangerous or assaultive in any way whatsoever. Nevertheless, the intern perceived him this way and thus was not an appropriate therapist for this patient.

A doctoral student that I was supervising also expressed some concerns about a patient she was seeing in therapy. In this instance, the patient was a very strong and muscular man who was in therapy because of a fear of losing control and possibly inflicting some physical damage on his supervisor. In this instance, with the support received from supervision, this young woman overcame her earlier fears and secured very positive results in about 16 sessions. This was an important, positive experience for her. However, without supervisory support and counsel, the case might not have gone so well.

Another comparable incident concerned a young colleague of mine who was the junior social worker in the clinic. As such, she didn't have a great deal to say about the cases assigned to her. She came to my office one day to discuss one particular paranoid patient and stated that she was very afraid of him. She also had a couple of other comparable cases and was reluctant to acknowledge her fears to her supervisor. In my judgment, such assignments were poor ones for both her and her patients. In some situations, perhaps, it may be difficult to make the best decision. In others, however, there may be no obstacles and it is up to the therapist to make an honest appraisal and be aware of his or her feelings with regard to the patient.

Lest the reader conclude that it is only fear that needs to be considered, I give two additional brief examples from my own experience. A young woman was referred to me who had difficulties in relating to men. In her first (and last) meeting with me, this young woman never ceased crying as she related her story. Although I consciously felt quite sympathetic to her, the peculiar manner she had of continuously crying as she spoke made me feel uncomfortable, and I decided that it was best to refer her elsewhere, perhaps to a female therapist. I gave her the names of three therapists I though would be more likely to help her.

My final illustration is of a young man who had a long history of very poor adjustment. He had failed at most things and had few desirable friends. In terms of the available information, he seemed like a poor candidate for psychotherapy. Consequently, I agreed to see him only on a provisional basis for evaluation. During our initial session, the young man's behavior and his accounts of past events were quite congruent with the information I had received and the preliminary judgments I had made. Nevertheless, underneath this individual's surface bravado and lack of concern I sensed a desire for contact and help. When I asked him what he thought he might get out of therapy, he replied that he might learn something, and he appeared quite sincere. Thus, although I considered that the prognosis was poor, I thought it worthwhile to see him once more before making a final decision. In this instance, some positive feelings toward the client clearly infuenced my decision.

It is apparent that the therapist must be an active, alert, and sensitive person in the initial session if the objectives of the session are to be attained. Not only must he or she carefully evaluate the problems presented, the degree of the client's pathology, and the personal strengths and weaknesses of the client, but the therapist must evaluate his or her personal reactions to the client and his or her interest in working with the client. There are other aspects of importance, such as the client's expectations and motivations concerning psychotherapy, which are discussed shortly. Here, the focus has been on the personality or personal qualities of the client and how the therapist responds to them.

CLIENT EXPECTATIONS

Clients come to psychotherapy with various views or expectations about it, and it is important that these be discussed and clarified. Otherwise, the two participants in therapy are entering a collaborative undertaking with two different expectations. Such a lack of congruence between the two participants is likely to present problems as therapy continues.

Ascertaining the client's views about therapy is therefore an important item in the initial interview and allows the therapist to clarify and explain what actually is involved. This does not require much time in most cases, but is a desirable procedure.

Some clients may come to therapy with expectations that closely resemble the therapist's. This may include such aspects as the frequency of therapy and the client's role in therapy. Others, however, may either be relatively uninformed or have some expectations derived from the movies or TV that are quite discrepant from those of the therapist. Consequently, it is worthwhile to clarify matters with the client before therapy gets underway. This can be done by explaining what therapy will consist of and the respective roles of the two participants, and then asking the client if this is what was anticipated. Conversely, the client can be asked about his or her expectations first, with the therapist then explaining what usually takes place. In both instances, however, it is important for the therapist to understand the client's expectations and for the client to understand what the process of therapy will entail. If, for some reason, the client does not want the kind of therapy the therapist offers, he or she is free to seek therapy elsewhere.

If the client has had previous therapy, it is worthwhile to find out precisely what occurred in the previous therapy. In this way, the therapist can mention any significant differences between the two therapies. It is also wise to go beyond a general designation for the previous therapy. For example, I agreed to see a woman for brief therapy who told me she had failed to be helped by her previous analysis. Because her husband was a physician and she was well educated, I took the analysis at face value. It was only during one of the therapy sessions that I discovered that her "analysis" had lasted for six sessions! In another situation, I agreed to take over a case from a psychiatric colleague who was leaving our clinic. This patient had been seeing the psychiatrist for over a year and a half without great change. Essentially, what I tried to do was to continue more or less where the previous therapist had left off. The therapy notes were quite brief, and after some discussion with the patient about the departure of the previous therapist and the nature of the patient's problems, I settled back to conduct therapy. After a half-dozen or so sessions, the patient verbalized his displeasure with my therapy and how it differed from his previous therapy. Although there were other factors involved here, we probably could have resolved the issues much more expeditiously if I had ascertained the patient's views of what actually went on in the previous therapy and then discussed my own approach with the patient. We eventually resolved the controversy, but it was not an easy matter and some time was wasted.

Some studies that I conducted in the past also convinced me that the therapist's expectations about therapy may be quite different from those of the client, and that it is better to find out what the client knows or expects than merely to conjecture about such matters (Affleck & Garfield, 1961; Garfield & Wolpin, 1963). Therapists, for example, always predicted that therapy would last longer than it actually did, whereas clients were closer to the mark. Clients, on the other hand, might have divergent views on other aspects of therapy. In one study, approximately half of the applicants for therapy thought each therapy session would last 30 minutes or less and a third of these patients thought some improvement or recovery would occur after two sessions of therapy (Garfield & Wolpin, 1963). Clearly, it would be wise to discuss such expectations before feelings of disappointment set in.

Even when we are quite cognizant of client differences, we still should not take too many things for granted. With clients of lower socioeconomic status and limited education, we obviously need to be sure we explain things adequately, in nontechnical language, concerning the process of psychotherapy and thus clarify clients' expectations. Sometimes individuals are referred for treatment who think of treatment in the medical sense and equate psychotherapy with being "crazy." In a case of this type, it is important to explain and clarify the situation. On the other hand, sometimes therapists are surprised by well-educated and highly intelligent persons whose expectations about psychotherapy are not what they had anticipated. At the end of an initial interview with an intelligent, expressive, and college-educated woman, I thought it best to inform her that, contrary to what I thought her expectations were, our therapy would be brief and probably not exceed 12 sessions. Somehow, I had the impression that she was anticipating long-term psychotherapy. To my surprise, she told me rather forcefully that she only planned on 5 sessions! Clearly, it is worth discussing such matters with the client at the beginning of therapy.

APPRAISAL IN TERMS OF THERAPY

As the initial session proceeds, the therapist tries to secure information that will allow him or her to make an adequate appraisal of the patient in terms of suitability for brief psychotherapy. The evaluation of the patient's problems, expectations about psychotherapy, personal strengths and weaknesses, as well as the therapist's own feelings about working with the patient, are all part of this overall appraisal. When the session ends, the therapist, in most instances, will make some decision relative to the acceptance or nonacceptance of the patient.

In order to obtain this objective, the therapist must direct and conduct the interview in an effective manner. Apart from the items already discussed, there are a few others that can be mentioned at this point. In addition to securing information about the client's problems, the duration of the problems, and any possibly related factors, it is also desirable to ask the client why he or she is seeking therapy at this time or why a referral was made now. Did something special occur? Such information may tell the therapist something about the client's motivation for therapy. For example, is the client seeking therapy now because his wife has threatened to leave him if he didn't get help? If so, what is his view about all this? If the client has made the decision himself, why has he made it at this time, particularly if the problem has existed for sometime? I recall seeing a patient many years ago who was seeking psychotherapy after he had received extensive physical examinations at a well-known university medical school and at the Mayo Clinic, both with negative results. The doctors could find nothing physically wrong, although he did have somatic complaints. This patient was finally giving psychotherapy a chance, but with relatively little enthusiasm.

It is also of interest to inquire about the client's view of his or her difficulties. Does the client have any opinions about why he or she has these particular difficulties or how they may have developed? Sometimes the client's views are informative and help the therapist round out his or her views of the client. They also may have implications for the therapeutic handling of the case. If the client believes that he or she is the victim of outside forces, the therapist may draw certain inferences. If the patient believes his or her symptoms are largely related to heredity, fate, or a bad horoscope, the therapist may draw other inferences.

As the initial interview draws closer to the end, the therapist basically is attempting to synthesize his or her information and observations of the individual. At least in a tentative way, the therapist will have attempted to evaluate the individual as a prospective therapy client, and in doing so will have weighed the positive, negative, and questionable features of the individual and viewed them in terms of some formulation about therapy. This process is not easy to describe, but I make a few comments about it. It is as if the therapist silently "says" some of the following comments:

This client's problems are rather severe, and I'm not sure if psychotherapy is the treatment of choice or if I can help her. I'm leaning toward referring her to Dr. Smith.

This client is a very insecure person but is intelligent and seems highly motivated to participate in therapy. He has also been successful in overcoming difficulties in the past. He is likeable and sincere. I believe I can work with him.

The problems presented by this person are not very serious, but the individual seems very dependent. This clearly will be a problem in therapy.

The problem here is really just a situational one that should respond quickly and successfully to a relatively few sessions. But participants have a lot going for them, are very pleasant, and should be able to handle the situation.

This bright young woman is depressed over the breakup of a recent relationship with a boyfriend. The depression is at least moderate, and this pattern has occurred before. She appears sincere about entering therapy, and a trial period seems warranted to appraise the depth of depression.

As the cognitive processing of the therapist proceeds in a manner such as this, the interview is nearing the end and the therapist is reaching some closure on a decision about the individual as a prospective client for psychotherapy. The therapist can suggest some other source of help to the individual, refer him or her elsewhere, or decide to accept the person on a regular or conditional basis. If the therapist has decided positively to accept the person for therapy, then the final part of the initial interview takes place and should be directed to orienting the prospective client to the psychotherapy that is to follow.

ORIENTING THE CLIENT TO THERAPY

The therapist, during the first therapy session, also needs to orient the client to what the psychotherapy process will be. As already indicated, one aspect is the ascertaining and clarification of the client's expectations about psychotherapy. In the preceding examples, the matter of the length of therapy was emphasized primarily because there was a significant discrepancy between the expectations of client and therapist. Such a discrepancy is undoubtedly less likely in brief psychotherapy. Nevertheless, it is still desirable to give the client some idea of the expected length of therapy, because this does involve time and money. However, other items of information also need to be provided to the client during the initial session.

Most clients who seek psychotherapeutic help tend to be quite concerned about the nature and seriousness of their problems. Consequently, it is important that the therapist say something about the frequency of occurrence and seriousness of the problems presented and also give the client some estimate of the relative prognosis. This is a very delicate area, because the therapist's knowledge and prognostications are far from perfect. Nevertheless, the therapist has some knowledge and research findings to fall back on and should strive to give as objective and valid information as possible. The therapist's effort should be an honest one; the therapist should not promise more than he or she can deliver nor be unduly pessimistic. Above all else, when the situation requires it, the therapist should admit whatever things are unclear as well as his or her inability to make a precise judgment or prediction. It is also a wise procedure to hold off or postpone making important decisions when the basis for making such decisions seems inadequate. The therapist can require an additional session if this seems reasonable. I have at times held off on some predictions or decisions by telling the client that I was unable to make such judgments at the end of the initial interview but that I would be better able to do so after about three or four sessions. Obviously, decisions are very much influenced by the particular client.

The therapist should also present the client with some brief overview of what will take place in therapy. Obviously, talking or verbal communication will constitute a large part of therapy, but therapy is more than just talk. Frankness and confidentiality in terms of what is discussed are matters that are worth emphasizing.

The client can be told that the therapy situation differs from most other situations and that it is important for the client to feel free to express his or her feelings and relate his or her troubles. Being able to discuss such matters may actually be helpful. Other more specific features of therapy will be determined by the nature of the client's problems. In the case of phobic behavior where the therapist may consider using systematic desensitization, some brief description of the process can be provided. If relaxation may be used as a possible coping method, a reference to the procedure can be made. The possible procedures to be used can be mentioned in a tentative manner, rather than stated definitively, to indicate some of the procedures that might be helpful. The purpose of providing such information is to give the client some idea of what actually will occur and to reduce ambiguity and distorted expectancies. Another benefit is that by indicating what will be occurring in therapy, the therapist indicates that he or she has some understanding of the problem and is able to plan the necessary steps that are likely to be helpful. This, in most instances, tends to foster confidence in the therapist and to increase hope in the client that he or she may be helped.

The therapist also should emphasize that psychotherapy involves and actually requires a collaborative relationship between therapist and client. Although the therapist will take an active and guiding role in therapy, it is essential that the client also play an active role. It is not just a matter of the client telling the therapist what is bothering him or her, along with the possible precipitating factors related to it, and then having the therapist tell the client what to do. Instead, the client must be willing to discuss important personal matters, thoughts, and feelings, even if they are upsetting, and to respond seriously to the explanations, questions, and assigments of the therapist. The client must be open about his or her experiences and feelings, including those pertaining to therapy and the therapist. Furthermore, working on the client's problems goes on outside of the therapy session, and this is a point well worth making. If changes are desired, then the client will have to cooperate with the therapist in working to secure change.

There are thus a number of important features of psychotherapy that need to be explained to the client in order for the client to be adequately oriented to what lies ahead and to his or her potential role in this process. In this way, the client is less likely to be surprised by what occurs and perhaps less likely to drop out of therapy prematurely. Furthermore, if the description of the therapy is not to the client's liking, it is better to have this matter settled before therapy proceeds any further than to have problems develop later. The client, in essence, can decide whether to continue in therapy or to go elsewhere, and the orientation and description have been open and honest.

ADMINISTRATIVE ARRANGEMENTS AND GROUND RULES

In addition to the activities already described, there are a few important practical matters that must be discussed if the therapist decides to accept the client for therapy. One such matter concerns the fee to be charged and how it is to be paid. How this is done will depend on the setting in which the therapist works. In clinical settings, this may be handled primarily by a secretary or receptionist with clear policies set by the clinic. In other situations, the therapist may be responsible for setting the fee. In some instances, a sliding fee scale is used with the fee determined in terms of the client's income and family status. Each therapist or each clinical situation determines what the fee policy will be. Whatever the policy, it is important that the matter of fees be discussed as well as the method of payment, so the client knows exactly what is required. Furthermore, if there are problems about the fee, it is best that they be discussed at the beginning and not become a problem that may intrude on therapy later.

Another matter that needs to be settled is that of agreeing on the time and date for the next meeting. Generally, it is a good procedure to select an appointment time that can also be used for future appointments. In this way, a specific time each week can be set aside by both participants and can be anticipated as the regular therapy time. This, of course, is not always possible and changes have to be made from time to time. However, I believe things proceed more smoothly and there is less confusion about meetings if a regular therapy time is used.

There are also a few other procedural matters that can be taken up in the initial interview. These are essentially ground rules governing some features of the therapy situation. For example, certain instructions or information can be given to the client about the possible need to cancel appointments (the importance of calling in advance when it is necessary to cancel or reschedule an appointment, for instance). Discussing the importance of being on time for the therapy session is another possible item. If deemed necessary, the client can be told that all sessions must end promptly, because the therapist has other appointments. How much the therapist wants to go into such matters will depend on both his or her evaluation of the client and personal preferences.

There may be some other minor informational items that may also come up in the first interview depending on the local setting. I have been asked about such matters as better routes to the clinic, parking facilities, health insurance, and related items. Although these are all items that appear peripheral to the main task of therapy, they may be important to particular clients. On the other hand, if the therapist notes a continued pattern of such requests from a particular client, the behavior in question takes on potentially more importance. In such an instance, the client may be exhibiting a regular feature of his or her personality that may reflect an overly dependent or demanding person. This aspect of the client's personality very likely could be related to the problems that bring him or her to therapy. Therefore, the therapist, at some point, instead of responding to the client's request, would want to point out this pattern of behavior and discuss its implications. However, this would tend to be done at a later time in therapy.

Toward the close of the session, it is also a good procedure to ask the client if he or she has any questions about any matters that have come up and have been discussed or about any other potentially relevant items. That the client has nodded affirmatively and asked no questions cannot always be taken as a sign of complete understanding. I have learned this from my own experience with both clients and students. In fact, I remember vividly the first experience I had of this type. During World War II, as a clinical psychologist in an army hospital, I was conducting a final interview with a soldier who was receiving a medical discharge on the basis of a psychiatric disorder. I, somewhat naively, thought it might be worthwhile to review with the soldier the things we had discussed previously concerning the factors that accounted for his symptoms and what had been wrong with him. As I went over this material, I frequently asked him if what I was telling him was clear. Each time he nodded his head and said, "It's very clear, Lieutenant." I must admit I felt very pleased and gratified with my performance. After his last "very clear, Lieutenant," I sat back contentedly and said we had covered everything. However, I asked him if there was any final question he might have before I said good-bye to him. He said he had only one question, and to my astonishment asked me, "What's wrong with me?"

Although the preceding example might be interpreted as indicating otherwise, I do believe that it is a worthwhile procedure to give the patient a chance to ask any final questions he or she may have about what was discussed or about psychotherapy generally. As emphasized already, it is best to reduce ambiguity and have as much mutual understanding as possible. Thus, if the therapist at any point feels the patient may not understand what is being discussed, he or she should ask if the patient has any questions and attempt to clarify the situation.

CONCLUDING COMMENTS

Some of the main features and objectives of the initial therapy session have been discussed. As indicated, the therapist must be active in securing the necessary information about the client and his or her difficulties, must observe astutely the behavior of the client in the interview situation, must evaluate his or her own reactions to the client, and then must make some overall appraisal in terms of the suitability of the client for brief psychotherapy. If the therapist concludes that the client is potentially suitable for therapy, he or she should use the remaining time to orient the client to what will be taking place and to the local ground rules. If a decision cannot be made during this initial interview, then an additional interview likely will be necessary to complete this process and allow for a decision to be made at that time.

Where a clinical or counseling setting has a limit on the number of sessions to be offered, the therapist has no problem in informing the client how long therapy will last. In non-time-limited brief therapy, the number of sessions may vary depending on the setting, the therapist, and the client. In most instances, the therapy usually will not exceed 20 sessions. Thus, the therapist can tell the client that therapy will consist of approximately 20 sessions or may require less. In my own practice, depending on the nature of the case, I may tell the client that therapy may last from about 12 to 20 sessions, and that after a few sessions we will be in a better position to know how many sessions are likely to be required.

Finally, for most individuals, the first session is a therapy session. I do not regard it strictly as an assessment session but as the beginning of therapy. Both participants have "sized up" each other and have entered into an initial agreement to collaborate in the psychotherapeutic undertaking. If the session has gone well, the client's hope of being helped has received some support, and his or her motivation for participating in therapy has correspondingly increased. The basis for developing a positive therapeutic relationship has been established, and the client has some understanding of the psychotherapeutic process that lies ahead. In general, the client should leave the first session somewhat encouraged and looking forward to the next therapy interview. After some concern about his or her symptoms, the client has taken the first step in attempting to do something about them, and the helping process has begun. The client has someone to turn to, and thus does not feel as troubled and isolated as before. In effect, some positive change may have already taken place.

Chapter 5

The Early Therapy Sessions

At the conclusion of the initial therapy session, the therapist needs to begin formulating some tentative plan for the therapy that is to follow. This need not be very detailed, nor is it necessary to adhere to it forever. However, it is desirable to have some plan or guide for therapeutic work. Essentially, the therapist highlights what he or she views as the client's main problem, the approaches or procedures that potentially will be most effective, and the possible difficulties that may be encountered as therapy progresses. In this manner, a tentative plan or map for the future therapeutic work is formulated. At the same time, it is recognized that this plan can, and quite likely, will be modified as the therapist learns more about the client in the sessions and interactions that follow. Thus, although the therapist is flexible in his or her formulations, what he or she attempts to do in the therapy sessions is not without direction.

In the previous chapter, particular emphasis was placed on the first therapy interview. A similar emphasis also is applicable to the early therapy sessions that follow. These sessions can confirm and strengthen positive views and expectancies acquired by the client in the first therapy session, remove possible doubts the client may have had about therapy, or have just the opposite effect. Somewhat comparable changes may also occur in terms of the therapist's view of the client and how therapy should proceed. Each participant has additional opportunities to observe and learn about the other member of the dyad. Original impressions thus are checked for possible confirmation, retraction, or modification.

As noted, in the first session each of the participants evaluates the other and comes to some decision about continuing the contact with additional sessions. On the part of the client, a decision is made that the therapist seems understanding and competent enough to offer some hope for help with the client's problems. The client's hopes are raised by a positive first impression, and the second session consequently is looked forward to with renewed hope and anticipation. It is very important, therefore, that this session proceed in a positive manner and that the expectations and motivation of the client are reinforced realistically by the interactions that take place. If the session proceeds smoothly, it is hypothesized that the motivation of the client to collaborate in the therapeutic endeavor is strengthened and, as a result, the formation of a positive therapeutic relationship begins to take place. In terms of what has already been discussed, this process is of the utmost importance.

Somewhat comparable processes occur with regard to the therapist. As mentioned, first impressions and hypotheses about the client and the probable course of therapy can be amended or revised based on additional information and observation. Although matters can still change noticeably as a result of additional sessions, the therapist begins to have more confidence in his or her appraisal of the client and in his or her formulations about treatment plans. The astute therapist should also be able to gauge how the client is responding to him or her and how the relationship is developing. If the therapist discerns any potential negative reactions on the part of the client, he or she should attempt to explore and clarify them. It is extremely important that open and honest communication take place and that disappointments and misinterpretations are expressed. The therapist's response, of course, should not be critical or overly defensive. The goal should be clarification in order that therapy proceeds on a basis of mutual understanding and trust.

The therapist has the opportunity in the early sessions to secure additional information, to clarify uncertainties and doubts, and to contribute to the establishment of a positive therapeutic relationship. His or her contribution to the development of a therapeutic relationship or therapeutic alliance is facilitated by a sincere interest in helping the client, by the therapist's understanding and empathy, and by a demonstration of competence. Above all, the therapist must be sincere and genuine in all interactions with the client. Phony behavior in any guise is usually sensed by the client and tends to undermine therapeutic collaboration and progress.

Consequently, the skilled therapist is particularly sensitive to behavioral reactions and cues from the patient in the early sessions. Any signs of uncertainty and dissatisfaction on the part of the patient need to be noted and, if possible, the underlying reasons ascertained. Not every item of the patient's expectations may have been discussed in the initial session, and some new experience may have occurred in the interval between sessions. Such new material, therefore, can be explored and earlier views modified accordingly. Because the early sessions to a large extent become the models for later sessions, it is important that any behaviors or patterns judged to be undesirable are responded to explicitly when they occur. Examples include being late to the session, lack of compliance on some assigned activity, or the patient's obvious contradiction of something related earlier. Although questioning the patient about such behaviors appears necessary to underline the importance of the behaviors involved for therapy, the therapist should not raise these questions in an accusatory manner. Rather, this can be done in a natural and businesslike way.

Such behavior by the therapist can also be viewed as concrete enforcement of the ground rules for therapy mentioned in the initial interview. In some ways, therapy can be seen as a two-person game with rules and responsibilities for both parties. When there are possible infractions on the patient's part, it is the therapist's responsibility to call them to the attention of the patient so that the behavior can be explained and modified. If they are allowed to go unnoticed early in therapy, they are more likely to be repeated with a possibly negative impact on the therapeutic process. I do not want to overemphasize this aspect or give it more prominence than it deserves; yet, for reasons already given, the activities and behaviors manifested in the early sessions are important for setting the patterns for later interactions and in establishing the therapeutic relationship.

Because this book has been written primarily for therapists and would-be therapists, it is perhaps understandable that the possible infractions or problematic behaviors of the client have been given primary attention. However, the therapist also may exhibit problematic behavior, and the blame cannot always and *should not* always be placed on the client or patient. I distinguish between two different types of problematic therapist behaviors. One pertains to the skills of the therapist, whereas the other category deals with issues of professional ethics.

Because therapists are not perfect and in fact show considerable variability in orientation, personality, experience, and skill, at times less than optimum therapeutic handling of a case will occur. Therapists should at least be aware of the possibility of such an occurrence. If therapy does not appear to be moving along satisfactorily, some self-reflection and evaluation may be in order, with consideration given to possible modifications. It may be that the therapist has incorrectly assessed the client's problems or has been insensitive to some aspects. Such problematic behaviors are not at all uncommon and are probably related to the therapeutic skills of the psychotherapist and the complexities of a given case. Therapists can always strive to do their best in their therapeutic work and yet realize that they will not always be as successful as they would like. This is a normal part of being a psychotherapist.

On the other hand, there are matters of professional ethics where all psychotherapists need to observe strict adherence. Therapists should not accept individuals for treatment who do not require such treatment or who are not likely to be really helped by means of brief psychotherapy. Although skill is involved in such decisions, most professionally qualified psychotherapists should be able to make such decisions. Consequently, I regard it as an ethical issue. Furthermore, if early in therapy the therapist is aware of unusually strong feelings toward the patient, whether positive or negative, he or she should seriously consider referring the case to another therapist. As previously noted, the therapist may be afraid of the patient. However, there are other cases where different problems may arise. Instances of strong sexual attraction, personal dislike of the patient, and marked differences in value systems or religious beliefs may also pose serious potential problems of an ethical nature for the therapist. Such potential problems may become reasonably clear in the early therapy sessions and are best handled at that time.

In the early sessions, therefore, the therapist cannot just sit back and listen to the client discuss his or her problems. The therapist must be actively involved in evaluating both the client's reactions as well as his or her own. There is also the process of securing additional information, extending observations, modifying initial hypotheses and evaluations, and formulating tentative treatment plans. Unless the therapist's perceptions of the client are significantly modified during these early sessions, the therapist will begin to have more confidence in his or her appraisal of the client and in his or her expectations about how therapy should proceed. In fact, if these sessions proceed smoothly, they auger well for the rest of therapy and the ultimate outcome. On the basis of some research, to be mentioned in the next section, it does appear that if the sessions have gone well and a good relationship between client and therapist has been formed, the chances for a successful outcome are increased.

THE EARLY SESSIONS
AND OUTCOME

Although the importance of the initial sessions of brief psychotherapy appears self-evident and has been emphasized in our discussion thus far, it is also worth mentioning some interesting research findings that bear on this topic. This research appears to indicate that although predictions about the course and outcome of psychotherapy usually cannot be made with great success after the initial interview, the situation is quite different by the end of the third therapy session.

Some years ago I and two colleagues conducted a study of first therapy interviews to see if we could predict duration of stay in psychotherapy (Garfield, Affleck, & Muffly, 1963). We attempted to investigate the relationship of certain variables pertaining to the patient, the therapist, and the patient-therapist interaction to therapy duration. The first therapy sessions of six therapists who each saw four new patients were tape recorded, and a variety of ratings were secured from patients, therapists, and the three investigators. Although there were a few suggestive findings, most of the ratings showed little relationship to continuation in psychotherapy. In light of the large amount of time and effort devoted to this project, the results discouraged me from further work of this kind. However, some more recent research in relation to outcome is distinctly more encouraging. Although the studies to be mentioned derive from two distinctly different orientations, there is a common thread that runs through the findings of both groups of studies.

In reviewing studies of client personality attributes and their relationship to therapy outcome, I noticed two studies that were particularly interesting (Garfield, 1986). In one study of participant modeling with snake phobics, "Neither initial attitudes toward snakes, severity of phobic behavior, performance aroused fears, nor fear proneness correlated with degree of behavior change" (Bandura, Jeffrey, & Wright, 1974, p. 62). However, there were measures of fear reduction taken after therapy had begun that were predictive of subsequent behavioral change. The greater the decrement during these early sessions, the greater the improvement. Somewhat comparable findings were reported in another study of 36 phobic patients (Mathews, Johnston, Shaw, & Gelder, 1974). Such client variables as severity of symptoms, level of anxiety and neuroticism, and low-rated motivation for treatment evaluated prior to treatment were not related to treatment outcome. However, similar to the finding reported by Bandura et al. (1974), those who subsequently improved showed a greater reduction in measures of rated anxiety early in therapy. Thus, the results secured in these two studies suggest that positive client changes early in therapy have prognostic significance for the ultimate outcome.

The other studies to which I refer come from investigations of the psychotherapy process conducted by psychodynamically oriented therapists and focusing mainly on the therapeutic alliance or helping relationship. Gomes-Schwartz (1978), in a study of therapy process variables predictive of eventual therapy outcome, secured the most promising results for a variable labeled as "patient involvement." This referred both to the patient's active participation in therapy and to manifestations of patient hostility. Patients who participated actively in therapy and manifested relatively little hostility early in therapy secured the best results. This study was based on data from the Vanderbilt research project and compared dynamically oriented therapists, experiential therapists, and college professors without psychotherapeutic training. For all three groups, comparable outcomes were secured and patient involvement was the best predictor.

In another study using the Vanderbilt Psychotherapy Process Scale, patient involvement again was found to have the highest relationship to outcome (O'Malley, Suh, & Strupp, 1983). However, of particular interest is that this relationship was not evident in the first therapy session. It only was clearly evident during the third session. Another psychotherapy process study of negative factors in psychotherapy also secured comparable results (Sachs, 1983). In this study, patient qualities, including negative attitudes and passivity, were significantly related to outcome when the ratings were based on the third therapy session but not on the first or second session.

In a study of the helping alliance, the most frequent positive helping alliance indicators in terms of outcome were those where the patients felt helped or changed (Luborsky, Crits-Christoph, Alexander, Margolis, & Cohen, 1983). What seems to be the important variable here is the patient's subjective feeling of positive change. As I noted in a recent review (Garfield, 1986):

> If one can view this as the patients' feeling better or seeing him or herself as improving early in therapy, then this early state of improvement may be indicative of positive outcome at termination. This view would also be congruent with the findings mentioned earlier by Bandura et al. (1974) and Mathews et al. (1974). The construct of patient involvement might also be related to the patient's feeling of being changed positively. The latter can act as a reinforcement for greater involvement in therapy. The fact that all of these related variables are not linked to outcome until the third interview also would appear congruent with this general hypothesis. (p. 246)

Regardless of how the therapist may want to conceptualize the basic variables operating during the first few sessions, and specifically the first three therapy sessions, it seems evident that changes can and do take place during these early sessions. Furthermore, if a positive collaborative relationship between client and therapist develops, the probability of some change or improvement during these sessions is enhanced. In addition, on the basis of the research findings just reviewed, it appears that such changes experienced early in therapy by the client also are a favorable indication for positive outcome at termination.

DISCERNING PATTERNS
OF BEHAVIOR

In the early sessions that follow the initial therapy interview, the therapist has the opportunity for additional observations of the client's behavior. This allows for a more valid appraisal of the client's interactions with the therapist. Initial impressions can be confirmed, rejected, or modified. Although the individual's patterns of reacting to specific situations usually will not vary a great deal, sometimes what is observable in a first interview may be influenced somewhat by cautious behavior on the individual's part. There may be some need to impress the therapist positively (or even negatively, on the part of some adolescents) in order to influence the therapist's decision concerning acceptance for therapy. Whether something of this kind has occurred or not, the therapist does increase his or her observational knowledge of the patient's behavior during the ensuing interviews and has a better "feel" for the patient. In essence, the therapist develops greater confidence in his or her knowledge of what kind of person he or she is working with in therapy.

The client's behavior in therapy is of critical importance for several reasons. Along with the verbal inputs provided by the client, the behavior exhibited during the interviews constitutes a basic source of information about the client. The client's typical ways of interacting with others can be inferred from the ways he or she interacts with the therapist. As mentioned earlier, clients show a large diversity of behavioral patterns in their interactions with the therapist. Some can be demanding, some can be self-deprecating and subservient, some can be quite ill at ease, some can be hostile, some can be passive, and so forth. To many therapists, the adage, "Behavior speaks louder than words" is exceedingly accurate. Consequently, not only do therapists learn more about the client as a person by observation of behavior but they also may gain a better understanding of the client's problems. It would be a rather unusual situation if the client's difficulties were not somehow intertwined with his or her behavior, or vice versa.

The client's behavior in the therapy situation also provides the therapist with information about how therapy is progressing and what may be potentially important problems for the therapeutic process. For example, a client who display some features of criticality and hostility early in therapy is more than likely to display such behavior in succeeding sessions, and the wise therapist is forewarned. Not only does such behavior constitute a very probable factor in the client's difficulties in interacting with others, but the same pattern will probably have to be dealt with in therapy for progress to be made. The therapy situation, although very special, brings forth typical learned behavior patterns on the part of the client. Unless the client deliberately acts out a role, he or she will behave and respond in therapy as he or she generally tends to behave when interacting with another person. Although social roles and situational status may influence the client's behavior in the initial session to some extent, more typical behaviors are the norm as therapy continues.

The therapist, during therapy, thus observes and deals with the usual and typical behaviors of the client. In contrast to psychodynamic therapists, I do not utilize the concept of transference or transference behavior, for I do not believe it is necessarily accurate or helpful in brief psychotherapy. Therapists do not need to distinguish between transference reactions (distorted behavior) and nontransference or reality-oriented behavior, because this brings in additional inferences and complications that are unnecessary. Certainly, the client behaves toward the therapist as he or she generally behaves toward other important figures in his or her life, and it is this behavior that is the focus here. Although the therapist may be able to infer hypothetically possible causal influences for the behavior observed, such inferences are not really necessary. If the behavior is problematic, then it needs to be modified if the client's level of adjustment is to be improved, and that is the task and goal of psychotherapy. Also, if the client is overly critical of the therapist, such criticisms need to be evaluated. If in fact they are not deserved, then the therapist can more confidently view this pattern of behavior as a likely problem of the client and try to deal with it in the therapy sessions. Obviously, if there is some justification for the client's critical behavior, then it suggests a problem deriving from the therapist's behavior, and this is quite another matter. For now, we concentrate on the client's behavior.

At this point, I provide the reader with some examples of the importance of observing the client's behavior and of responding to it in an appropriate manner. Again, it is important to stress that the client's behavior provides clues concerning both the client's real-life problems and his or her attitudes toward therapy and the therapist. Although these are clearly interrelated, for purposes of exposition it is worth viewing them separately.

I start with a relatively obvious case that I saw when I was working in an outpatient clinic. This individual, a 40-year-old man with two years of college, was first interviewed and tested by a postdoctoral intern, for whom the experience was almost traumatic. The patient was continuously critical of almost everything she did or said, and when she lit up a cigarette in her state of tension, he accused her of being an addict. I was more fortunate than the intern was because I was older, a male, and of higher status in the clinic. Also, I was forewarned by her experience. Nevertheless, I knew that my meetings with this patient would not be easy. Although my initial therapy session with him was much less troublesome than the one the intern had experienced, it was not easy. The patient was very critical and hostile and, not surprisingly, had severe difficulties in getting along with others. Even when he asked questions and wasn't attacking me verbally, his questions seemed like accusations.

This individual clearly presented serious difficulties for the therapist. First of all, the therapist would have to strive not to be defensive and overreactive to the behaviors of the patient. The therapist also would have to keep in mind continuously that the patient was a troubled and unhappy person whose behaviors made helping him very difficult. Developing a positive and collaborative therapeutic relationship would not be an easy task, because the patient appeared to have little trust in others and was an expert in making others avoid him.

This patient, in the first therapy session, although not overly critical of me, did offer very strong criticism of the intern. However, hostile remarks and comments were more forthcoming in the subsequent interviews. Therapy actually was a stormy affair, with several self-terminations by the patient and as many self-initiated returns to therapy over a period of a few years. The case is cited here to illustrate that the problem behavior, for both patient and therapist, was apparent early in therapy. The patient's behavior was also something that the therapist was able to indicate to the patient as a concrete manifestation of his difficulty with others. In this instance, therapy was more than just words—there was a focus on the actual behavior of the patient, and this does have a real impact.

Pointing out problematic behaviors to the client is not always easy to do. Because such comments are easily perceived as criticisms of the client, some therapists are reluctant to make them for fear of alienating the client. In my opinion, these therapists are not using the opportunities for possible patient change afforded by focusing on the client's behavior. At the same time, it must be admitted that such a focus on the client's behavior must be done with a great deal of sensitivity. It cannot be carried out in a critical or defensive manner if it eventually is to have a therapeutic impact. What the therapist must communicate is that he or she is pointing to behaviors that contribute to the client's difficulties and that therefore need to be changed. This can be done in a noncritical manner and accepted by the client without undue negative effect. Where the client's behavior directly impacts on the therapy situation in terms of such matters as being late or cancelling appointments, it is essential that the client be confronted with these matters when they occur, and particularly if they occur early in therapy. Where the behavior in question is viewed as a more general part of the client's problem, it may be desirable to postpone comments until more of a relationship has been established between therapist and client.

An illustration of the preceding point is my therapy with a man who exhibited problems of a passive-aggressive type. He constantly verbalized critical comments of all the people with whom he came in contact. According to his accounts, no one ever treated him fairly and everyone tried to exploit him. At the same time, he was overtly obsequious and deferential to me, even bringing gifts during holidays. Despite this pattern of deference to me, in several ways he subverted what I was trying to accomplish in psychotherapy by privately and secretly getting special medical examinations and seeking medical treatment. When all of this came to light later, I was able to use his own behavior with me, as well as with others, in pointing out the problems he created for himself. Being aware of his behavior early in therapy, I was easily able to refrain from accepting his gifts and thus could not be accused of also exploiting him. Later, I was able to help him see how he created situations that essentially allowed him to view others as exploitative. By gradually changing his behavior, he also discovered that most people weren't really trying to take advantage of him.

Other types of behavioral patterns reflecting the personalities of the clients seeking therapeutic help also can be noted by the psychotherapist. The patterns of behavior are only limited by the range of human psychopathology and personality. As already indicated, some clients are hostile and critical, whereas at the other extreme some appear to be overly deferential. Some talk a great deal and some talk very little. Some talk of inconsequential matters, whereas some seem to discuss really important matters. Some joke and laugh; some are tearful and cry. Some arrive for their sessions early, whereas others always seem to miss the bus or can't find a parking place. I have had some patients who appeared seductive, and I recall one patient who liked to play with a hunting knife during the few therapy sessions I had with him. In all of these instances, therapists have the opportunity of observing the behavioral patterns of clients that are truly meaningful. These observations inform the therapist of important components of the client's problems, they alert the therapist to possible difficulties that may be encountered in the therapeutic work with the client, and they also provide the therapist with specific concrete material that can be used in trying to secure client change.

MODIFYING EARLIER IMPRESSIONS

As previously indicated, the therapist's overall impression of the client based on referral information and the initial interview may have to be modified as the therapist conducts additional sessions with the client. Certain aspects of the client's personality and behavior may come into sharper focus as therapy gets under way. Earlier formulations and tentative plans for therapy accordingly may have to undergo change. Where there is a very clear main problem, such as a specific phobia, and an available effective form of treatment, such as gradual exposure to the anxiety-provoking stimulus, no great changes are required. However, where the problems are less specific and less clear initially, some changes or additions to the planned work with the client may be required. This is also the case where the client's main problem is not presented until after a few therapy sessions have occurred and the client has gained sufficient trust in the therapist.

What appears important in these early sessions is the therapist's sensitivity to the client and his or her problems. The therapist may see that statements may have to be made more tentatively to some clients and more positively to others. Some clients, for example, may take everything the therapist says very seriously, including an attempt to be humorous. Other clients, however, may seem to respond in quite an opposite manner, and this requires a more forceful response or manner from the therapist.

There is nothing particularly unusual or surprising about the need on the part of the therapist to retain flexibility and to be able to modify impressions and judgments as further experience with the client is secured. Effective therapists have always been adaptable to the per-ceived needs of the therapy situation. However, at the same time, it is also apparent that some therapists seemingly follow some set of previously acquired guidelines regardless of the need to modify proce-dures to meet changing circumstances. This is, perhaps, more likely to occur where the therapist is a strict adherent to one form of psycho-therapy than where the therapist is more eclectic in orientation or where the therapist is relatively inexperienced.

Although I stress the sensitivity of the therapist and the need for the therapist to be able to change his or her view of the client's problems and early treatment plans, I do not promote the model of a constantly changing therapist who "flies by the seat of his pants." On the contrary, it is essential that the therapist be viewed by the client as a steady and reliable source of hope and support. There clearly must be consistency and continuity. However, this does not signify rigidigy and forcing the client to adhere to the therapist's plan regardless of its suitability. Even though the therapist may change his or her earlier impressions of what is required in therapy, the therapist's interest, empathy, and sensitivity for the client should not vary.

I recall the case of a 50-year-old woman whose husband had suddenly left her. She was quite depressed and tearful and appeared rather devastated by this unexpected action of her husband. I felt that the therapist whom I was supervising, should be quite supportive and allow the patient to ventilate her feelings. The patient verbalized her feelings quite freely, and this pattern seemed to be worthwhile during the first two sessions. During the next two sessions, however, we received a different impression of the patient. She didn't appear as depressed as previously and completely dominated the session, in some ways intimidating the student therapist. It was necessary to modify our view of the patient and also to have the therapist take over control of the situation. The patient, in this instance, was not as traumatized and incapacitated as we inferred at the beginning of therapy. We also had a better understanding of her interpersonal behavior, both for problems in conducting her therapy and in terms of her marital difficulties. The patient's need to dominate others thus became apparent as a critical item that needed to be handled in therapy and eventually in her own life situation.

This discussion of the possible need to modify initial impressions of the client may appear to be in opposition to the recent trend to develop therapy manuals for specific kinds of psychotherapy. The implication of this latter development is that there are specific therapies that can be taught, and that such manuals will ensure comparable behaviors on the parts of the therapists. In attempting to evaluate and compare different forms of psychotherapy, such manuals have appeared to promise, to some extent, that therapists of one school will deliver the therapy as described in the manual. Because we can't be sure what kind of therapy a therapist actually conducts by the therapy designation he or she provides, using a training manual would tell us much more about the therapy conducted and also guarantee greater similarity of performance.

Although it is undoubtedly true that therapy manuals may increase the similarity of those who are trying to perform a specific form of therapy, particularly if they are part of a research project, this by no means signifies that therapists will be exactly alike or equally skillful. To the extent that psychotherapy involves the personal qualities of the therapist and is not simply a matter of techniques, it must always allow for personal variability even among practitioners of the same school of psychotherapy. Furthermore, because patients with the same diagnosis will also differ in many personal respects, therapists, to be maximally effective, must be flexible and adapt their approach to the needs of the patient. When their perception of a patient also changes as therapy gets under way, they must modify their approach accordingly.

SENSITIVITY TO PROBLEMS

Although some references to possible problems in therapy have been made in preceding sections, this matter deserves additional commentary. Depending on the therapist's selection criteria and the types of clients he or she works with, a majority of clients will show some positive movement in therapy. However, therapy will not always proceed smoothly, and problems may arise from time to time. The therapist must be particularly sensitive to problems that emerge early in therapy, because they can have an important influence on the course of therapy.

We have already commented very briefly on such obvious potential problems as being late for the therapy session, cancelling appointments, failing to pay the therapist's fees, and similar matters. There are also other types of more or less obvious problems to which the therapist must be sensitive. Regardless of their nature, any signs of potential problems noted early in therapy require some type of appropriate response on the part of the therapist.

We first discuss some of the more obvious problems. How should the therapist respond when the client has been late to the first few sessions? First of all, it is necessary to look at the specific facts and see if there is some pattern. Has the client been late to every session? How late has he been in each instance? I give the client the benefit of the doubt when the amount of lateness is small and there are easily discernible reality factors accounting for such a pattern, for example, real parking problems. Before jumping to conclusions about unconscious resistance factors, the therapist must first rule out reality factors. On the other hand, when the client has consistently arrived more than 10 minutes late for each session and the reasons each time appear somewhat fanciful, the therapist cannot ignore such a pattern. An obvious question is why 20% or more of the therapeutic session is being wasted. Another question would be whether or not the client always exhibits such a pattern in going to work, attending meetings, or going to classes. If this pattern appears specific to therapy, then issues concerning therapy should be explored.

If the pattern is a more generalized behavioral pattern, the implications of such behavior for the client's overall adjustment and the possible reasons for it should be sought. In the latter instance, as indicated earlier, the therapist has an opportunity to point to specific behaviors that have real-life implications for the client.

The therapist must clearly differentiate between what is regarded as polite and socially acceptable behavior and behavior that is called for in light of the therapeutic situation. Relatively inexperienced therapists may feel it is somewhat undignified or socially inept to make an issue of the client's being late. I hope the preceding illustration makes clear that this view is incorrect in terms of therapy, and that holding such a view will cause the therapist to lose opportunities for more effective treatment.

Another potential problem that may occur with some patients early in therapy is that of missed or cancelled appointments. I differentiate between these two categories of absence by stating that cancelled appointments are those where the client phones in ahead of the scheduled appointment and states that he or she will be unable to keep it. Usually, the client will give some reason, such as illness, and will indicate that he or she hopes to be well enough to make the session next week. In most instances, such cancellations can be accepted for what they are. All of us have things that come up, such as our own illness or illness of a family member, which may cause us to cancel and reschedule an appointment. Of course, there may be an occasional bizarre pattern of 10 successive cancellations that have to be viewed in a somewhat different light. However, such instances are rare.

Missed appointments, or where the client fails to show up for a scheduled appointment without any prior notification, is another matter altogether. This must be viewed seriously, especially when it occurs early in therapy. Unless there is a truly adequate explanation for such behavior, the therapist must view it as a manifestation of the client's lack of interest and involvement in therapy. Consequently, if the client returns for the following or a subsequent session, the therapist must make the missed appointment the first order of business. By discussing this issue, the therapist attempts to ascertain the causes of the missed appointment and also communicates to the client the serious implications of such behavior.

Lack of client involvement, as manifested in the failure to keep therapy appointments, is also a possible indicator of premature termination from therapy. In a study of 91 clients seen at the Psychological Service Center at Washington University, missed appointments were correlated significantly with premature dropouts from psychotherapy (Berrigan & Garfield, 1981). This was not the case with reference to cancelled appointments. Thus, missed appointments definitely should be seen as a more significant problem than cancellations. Of the 28 clients in this study who missed one or more therapy sessions, almost half terminated therapy prematurely. In contrast, less than one fifth of the 63 clients who did not miss a session terminated prematurely. Furthermore, clients in the two lowest social class categories of the Hollingshead Index had very high rates of premature termination. Consequently, the therapist must be particularly sensitive to how such clients respond to the early sessions of therapy.

When the client has failed to appear for a scheduled therapy session, the therapist has several possible alternatives. The therapist can wait for a few days to see if the client calls to offer some explanation and signifies that he or she plans on coming to the next appointment. The therapist or the therapist's secretary can call the client a day or two later to see about scheduling the next appointment. The therapist can have a letter sent stating that the client was missed but that the regular appointment time is being reserved for the client, and the therapist looks forward to seeing the client at that time. Or the therapist can do nothing and leave the initiative up to the client. I know of no studies in this area that can provide adequate guidance for the therapist. In some instances, the therapist's appraisal of the client may suggest one type of action rather than another. I generally refrain from contacting the client by phone or letter but hold open the appointment time for the following week. If the client fails to show up or make arrangements to come in at that time, I send him or her a letter stating that I interpret failure to keep appointments as a sign that the client doesn't want to continue in therapy at this time. I also add a statement that should the client feel otherwise in the future, he or she should feel free to contact me.

In the case of students seeing their first clients in a practicum or internship, I have been more flexible in handling missed appointments. Such therapists in training tend to be very involved with their cases and will do almost anything to avoid having one of them drop out of therapy. Consequently, I have allowed some of them to phone their recalcitrant clients and to check their next appointment with them. However, I very clearly have counseled them against offering the client any inducement to come in for future therapy sessions, much as some of them seemingly would like to do. I have also followed the procedure of having the student send a letter to the client after two successive missed appointments, as described earlier.

Having a patient who supposedly needs psychological help drop out of therapy prematurely is a negative experience for practically all psychotherapists, not just for therapists in training. Over the years, the therapist may harden somewhat against such occurrences, but they do have potential implications for the therapist's professional ego. It is also difficult to objectively evaluate such incidents in terms of possible causative factors. For example, as indicated, patients of low socioeconomic status have been found to drop out of psychotherapy at a greater rate than do patients of high socioeconomic status. The therapist who works with large numbers of such patients should be aware of the research findings on this matter and should try to adapt his or her psychotherapy accordingly. At the same time, research studies also indicate that if lower social class patients continue in therapy, they do approximately as well as other patients (Garfield, 1986).

A conscientious therapist, therefore, should try to evaluate his or her own cases of premature termination in order to provide possible clues for understanding this phenomenon and reducing the incidence of such cases. In this process, it is important to avoid placing all the blame on the patient or on the therapist.

In a different type of situation that sometimes occurs, there is also a need for sensitivity on the therapist's part. I refer to those instances where a patient shows sufficient improvement, in terms of his or her presenting problem, to be considered for termination after only a few psychotherapy sessions. As indicated in chapter 1, it has taken at least a few years for brief therapy of 20 to 25 sessions to be recognized and accepted as a worthwhile and respectable pursuit. For some therapists, acknowledging that some patients may be helped sufficiently in three, four, or five sessions is difficult; yet my own experience, as well as some research, indicates that this does in fact occur. A recent report of studies on "The Dose-Effect Relationship in Psychotherapy" stated that approximately one third "of the patients improved within the first three sessions, regardless of the ultimate duration of treatment" (Howard et al., 1986, p. 160). A somewhat larger percentage improved between the fourth and seventh therapy sessions. Furthermore, these cases were seen in what might be called regular unlimited therapy and not for brief or time-limited therapy. These data, therefore, lend some empirical support to the view that some clients may indeed show meaningful improvement in a very brief time and with a minimal number of sessions. Practicing therapists, therefore, at least should be aware of this possibility.

I recall two cases of my own where one session of therapy was deemed sufficient, one case where four sessions sufficed, and three cases where therapy was concluded at the end of five sessions. I admit that in most of these cases I did not enter therapy with such a treatment goal in mind. However, the termination in each case seemed reasonable to me, and I did not put any pressure on these clients to continue except to let them know I could be contacted in the future. Some clinicians might want to call some of these contacts consultation rather than therapy, but as far as I was concerned the clients came in with a problem and were helped with it sufficiently so that no additional sessions were required. Even where one primarily practices brief psychotherapy, the client's expectations may be less than those of the therapist, or a positive outcome may be secured more quickly than anticipated by either participant.

Nevertheless, because most clients who begin a course of psychotherapy appear to require more than just a few sessions, many or perhaps most therapists might encourage the client to continue despite the client's improvement and desire to terminate. Psychodynamic therapists have referred to a client's unusually quick improvement as a "flight into health." From this point of view, an unexpected and sudden disappearance of the client's symptoms signifies that the client is defending him or herself against the probing for and possible emergence of unconscious material by becoming "healthy" and no longer requiring therapy. This is really the ultimate form of resistance, because it allows the client to remove him or herself from the threat of therapy. From this point of view, the therapist must not be deceived by these maneuvers of the client but must interpret this behavior to the client in the hope of keeping him or her in therapy.

I obviously do not adhere to such a view. I am inclined to accept the clients' reports of how they are feeling and getting along unless I have some very good reasons for not doing so. There are instances where a client may say he or she is getting along satisfactorily but says it in a manner that contradicts his or her words or adds a qualifier such as "OK, I guess." The therapist doesn't have to be an intuitive genius to judge that such individuals are not greatly improved. I do not discuss such cases here, because there is no insistence in these cases that the client's symptoms or complaints have disappeared or greatly improved. Rather, I discuss the latter type of case and give a brief example. In this case, a patient's fear of possibly harming a family member cleared up by the third interview, and after the fourth session it was decided mutually to terminate therapy. The patient was told to contact the therapist should his symptoms return. My colleagues at the time pronounced this case as a flight into health. However, this patient never called back over a two-year period and seemingly was no longer bothered by his specific fear. I was quite willing to accept the improvement in this case and hoped that a few other of my cases would have a flight into health.

There are other reasons that therapists sometimes may be reluctant to terminate clients after only a few sessions. Such behavior may be contrary to their expectations; they may have too many open hours or, in the case of students, too few clients; they may be practicing a form of time-limited therapy that requires a specified number of interviews; or there may be a particular personal involvement with a specific client. Needless to say, the therapist should be aware of such motivations and recognize that he or she is sacrificing the client's needs to his or her own. Prolonging treatment unnecessarily, even where the total expected treatment is relatively brief, is still an undesirable and essentially unethical procedure. Brief psychotherapy, or long-term psychotherapy for that matter, does not imply or guarantee that a client who completes a course of therapy will never again need psychotherapy. In fact, the available data are to the contrary (Sloane et al., 1975). Thus, it is a reasonable and warranted procedure to terminate therapy when improvement occurs more rapidly than expected, and it is also reasonable to believe that clients may again seek relatively brief periods of psychotherapy in the future, with the same or even a different therapist, with positive outcomes.

Although it may be surprising to some psychotherapists that individuals with problems or symptoms serious enough to warrant seeking professional help should improve so rapidly, there are several possible reasons for such rapid improvement. Some individuals will seek professional help when the problems are minimal, whereas some literally have to be dragged to the professional's office when they are already in critical condition. Thus, some individuals with not so serious problems may improve rapidly. A second possible explanation for some clients is *spontaneous recovery*. This designation has been used in medicine to indicate that an individual has recovered from an illness without the help of any specific therapeutic regimen—for example, a long-time chronic psychotic patient provided only with custodial care suddenly appears lucid and normal. Spontaneous recovery, of course, can occur in less severe disorders, and some critics of psychotherapy have claimed that the improvements secured by means of psychotherapy are in reality due to spontaneous recovery.

Another possible explanation of quick improvement in psychotherapy is the occurrence of an important change in the client's social or interpersonal situation. For example, a break-up in a close relationship may lead individuals to become depressed and to seek psychotherapeutic help. If during the first few sessions the previous relationship is restored or a new one begun, the depression may lift fairly quickly. I do not make light of the help provided by the psychotherapist in such cases, for the therapist has helped the individual to get over a stressful and unhappy episode in his or her life.

There are a number of other possible problems that may become more apparent in the early sessions and to which the therapist should be sensitive. If the patient should appear to be more disturbed than originally thought, the therapist needs to evaluate the situation very carefully and decide if a consultation or referral is appropriate. If what initially seemed to be mainly an internalized or individual-centered problem begins to look more like a marital problem, the therapist may want to rethink his or her original goals and plans and seriously consider having the client's spouse also participate in the therapy. If the client seems to add little new information of consequence or seems to be sitting back and awaiting the therapist's directions and comments, the therapist may have to explore with the client what is occurring. A similar response on the part of the therapist may be called for if the client says, in passing, that therapy is not what he or she expected or that progress seems very slow.

The therapist also should be sensitive to certain patterns that have implications for modifying his or her approach or for additional probing to explain the particular pattern. For example, some patients may say little of consequence during the session, but when the therapist says "our time is up," they begin to relate something of importance. In one case that I was supervising, the client appeared to continue a discussion from the previous session that was in no way unusual, but at the end of the session when she reached the office door, she unexpectedly remarked to the therapist that she had been thinking of suicide! This was a complete surprise to the student and left her completely bewildered. When something like this happens, the therapist experiences a real conflict between wanting to give the additional time and terminating the session as scheduled. The therapist must evaluate the situation very quickly in order to respond in the most appropriate manner. In most situations where the client brings forth important material near the end of the session, an appropriate response is to acknowledge the significance of the client's statements and to tell him or her to be sure to bring this up at the beginning of the next session. In this way, the therapist makes clear that the therapy hour is the time to discuss things and that the time limits are to be observed. Where, as in the example cited, the client's statement is of a very serious nature, the therapist must evaluate the client's state and decide accordingly. In some instances, it may be wise to give the client some additional time in order to make an accurate clinical judgment. In others, it may seem prudent to have the client call a day or so later; in other instances only the comment about discussing the client's feelings at the start of the next session may be required.

The early sessions of therapy thus call for considerable sensitivity on the part of the therapist. He or she must be alert to all possible behaviors and cues that potentially may be forthcoming or discernible during the therapeutic interactions. Sometimes, the earliest impressions become confirmed and therapy proceeds in a largely anticipated manner. In other instances, unexpected developments may appear that require rethinking and reformulations on the therapist's part.

HOMEWORK ASSIGNMENTS
AND SELF-MONITORING

During the early sessions of psychotherapy, the therapist may also decide to make use of homework assignments including self-monitoring. These procedures, derived largely from cognitive-behavior therapy and contrary to client-centered and psychodynamic views, have potential utility with selected patients. Although I have not used them as frequently or systematically as have behavior therapists, I have found them helpful with some of the clients I have seen, and a few examples follow.

Among the current procedures used to help individuals with symptoms of anxiety, tension, and even hypertension is training in relaxation. In addition to the learning that can take place during the weekly therapy hour, there are opportunities for learning and practice during the many remaining hours in the week. Not only can a considerable amount of practice and learning take place outside of the therapist's office, but much of it can occur in the more realistic social environment in which the client lives. If relaxation is also taught as a coping technique to help in meeting problematic situations, practice at some point in actually coping with a real situation can be very therapeutic when performed successfully.

In a few instances where the major problem of some male clients was a lack of confidence in meeting and relating to women, I have used some very simple assignments that seemed to contribute to the total outcome of treatment. For example, in one instance I had the client seat himself during lunch at a table occupied primarily by women. He was to become engaged in appropriate conversation and repeat this procedure when possible. According to this client's self-report, this procedure did increase his confidence and reduce his timidity in relating to women. There are a large number of possible variations on this theme that clinicians can devise and adapt to the needs of particular clients. As already emphasized, however, it is most desirable to discuss such possible assignments with the client and secure his or her suggestions and cooperation. Forcing an activity on a client who responds very negatively to the suggested assignment is counterproductive. However, in such a case, the client's opposition to the therapist's suggestion would appear to indicate the presence of a serious problem in the therapeutic relationship—and this problem would have to be investigated and rectified before any other matters could be handled with any degree of success.

Having clients keep a diary or self-monitor certain occurrences is also a procedure that can be initiated during the early therapy interviews. Such procedures can be applied in a variety of cases. If a client is vague about how frequently certain events occur or what kinds of situations seem to trigger certain arguments or emotional states, an assignment to record all such incidents with sufficient descriptive data can be proposed to the client. Similarly, couples seen in marital therapy can be asked to record items that appear to trigger serious arguments, to record behaviors of the spouse that are considered troublesome as well as loving and supportive, and similar types of items. Individuals who are overweight and desirous of slimming down as either a primary problem or as an associated problem can be asked to record everything they eat in terms of quantity, time, and circumstance. Such recordkeeping or self-monitoring can actually serve several purposes. It should provide more accurate data than simple narrative recall, it can mirror very specifically for the client how much he or she eats, and over a period of time it can inform the client if progress is actually being made. If the latter is actually occurring, this can act as a type of meaningful reinforcement.

The variety of tasks or assignments that can be used by psychotherapists is undoubtedly limited only by the type of problem and the creativity of the therapist. However, the tasks themselves must be seen as meaningful by the client and as a means of trying to overcome the difficulties for which he or she has sought therapy. Because so many individuals have developed a negative attitude toward homework, it is important to point out the relevance of the assigned task or what is to be practiced for the goals of therapy. Also, as indicated earlier, it is important to have the client participate in planning the homework or in expressing his or her reactions to it.

The tasks or activities assigned should have a better than average probability of being completed successfully. Even though successful experiences cannot always be secured, the possibility of a serious consequence due to failure must be considered carefully. A person who has severe social anxiety should not be asked to perform interactions that may only decrease his or her anxiety threshold and perhaps increase his or her pessimism about treatment. In general, the nature of assignments during the early interviews should not be overly demanding or stressful. Assignments should follow a graded pattern or hierarchy comparable to that used in systematic desentization, with the more difficult assignments coming after successful performance on the earlier and less demanding assignments.

It is also desirable to have the client note down the results of his or her attempts to practice the behavior assigned and the feelings he or she experienced during and after their occurrence. These can be discussed at the following therapy session and responded to as deemed appropriate by the therapist. The therapist should bestow adequate praise on the client for successful performance, because this is not only justified but it also reinforces the client's collaborative work in therapy. Any assignment should be discussed, and whatever changes are deemed desirable should be made. The client can be praised for attempting to carry out the assignment and encouraged to attempt the next week's modified assignment. As always, the therapist must evaluate the impact of what was done and to modify his or her procedures if required.

FLEXIBILITY OF APPROACH

As indicated, the therapist must evaluate the interactions that are taking place in the therapy sessions. Based on these evaluations, the therapist may find it necessary to modify his or her earlier formulations and to plan new approaches and procedures. There is no set of hard-and-fast rules that can be followed in a prescribed way for each patient, even when they may appear to have the same presenting complaint or diagnosis. Schofield (1988), in a recent book, held a similar view and offered the following comment:

> Except for specific aspects of behavior modification or behavior therapy, the conduct of psychotherapy is not a technology. There are no rule books that direct the therapist as to when and how to apply prescribed interventions: "If condition A, use technique B," or "When X occurs, stop Q and switch to Z." . . . the therapist is not a computer who serves simply as a processor to assure a fixed transformation from "stimulus in" to "response out." (pp. 128–129)

The lack of a precise and ordered set of rules and procedures that can be followed easily by the psychotherapist provides a considerable disappointment to students beginning their training in psychotherapy. Wouldn't it be nice if there were a psychotherapy manual that was as specific as those developed in the past for the Standford-Binet or Wechsler Scales of Intelligence? It would certainly make life easier for both students and their instructors. However, the reality of the situation is otherwise, and the effective therapist is aware of this. I know from my own experience how graduate students and beginning therapists desire a concrete guidebook that would spell out everything that the therapist needs to do and in the prescribed order. Recently, after delivering a lecture on psychotherapy at a large teaching hospital, I met for a while with a group of psychology interns. Very few of their questions dealt with topics I had covered in my lecture. Rather, their questions were concerned mainly with techniques and procedures of psychotherapy. The questions reflected their current problems with the patients they were seeing. Although I couldn't give them concrete answers that would apply to all their cases, I did try to reassure them that their uncertainties would diminish gradually as they gained experience and that it was desirable to maintain an open mind. A premature fixation on one therapeutic approach without being open to other ideas is comparable to closing the cerebral arteries.

Admittedly, it is difficult and anxiety provoking at times to have to continually evaluate the process of psychotherapy in which you are the psychotherapist. It is more comforting to have explicit rules to follow and to know (believe) that by adhering to these rules you are actually providing the best service for your patient. This is one reason that people learn and follow a specific approach to psychotherapy, even when it may not be a truly valid or effective system. This is epitomized in an illustration provided by Jerome Frank of a young psychiatric resident who remarked that one of the main advantages of practicing psychoanalysis was that even when a patient did not get better, you knew that you had provided the very best therapy.

In the real world, however, the effective therapist must be flexible and adapt to the needs and personality of the individual patient. Flexibility is called for, not rigidity. It is a testimonial to the astuteness and integrity of perhaps the majority of psychotherapists that they tend to become eclectics, modifying and changing their views as they gain in experience (Garfield & Kurtz, 1976). At the same time, this attempt to broaden views and adapt procedures to the individual patient's requirements should not lead to practice that is not guided by reflection, planning, and reasoned implementation. Practice clearly should not consist of a haphazard application of techniques. Instead, the therapist must rely on his or her best judgment of what is required in the specific instance and draw on his or her knowledge and past experience. When earlier judgments seem to require change on the basis of additional work with the patient, a careful rethinking and possible change in procedure are likely required. This considered flexibility is the mark of a skilled and responsible professional therapist. It may be required during the early sessions of psychotherapy, and it also may be required during other stages of therapy. Throughout therapy, the psychotherapist must be sensitive and responsive to the interactions that take place in the therapy session.

Chapter 6

The Middle or Interim Phase of Therapy

As emphasized in the preceding chapters, the first few sessions of psychotherapy are exceedingly important and set the stage for what is to follow. They provide an opportunity for additional client assessment, for initial treatment planning, for indicating possible problems in therapy, and for developing a positive therapeutic relationship or alliance between therapist and client. For a certain percentage of patients, the early sessions will actually constitute the entire amount of therapy received. Some will simply fail to return for a scheduled appointment after the first, second, or third therapy session, and in most of these instances the therapist may not know the real reason for this failure to reappear. In a small number of such cases, the clients will state that they seemed to be doing better and thus saw no need to continue with therapy. There may also be a small number who have terminated therapy with the concurrence of the therapist because of apparent improvement. In this latter instance, improvement may be due to the resolution of a crisis or to a positive change in the client's life situation.

After the third or fourth interview, the probability of premature termination diminishes. Furthermore, as discussed earlier, if a good collaborative relationship has been established and it appears that the client is making some progress, the prognosis for continuation and a favorable outcome is enhanced. The sessions begin to take on a more settled and familiar appearance, and the main work of therapy has begun.

As the middle or interim phase of psychotherapy gets under way, both participants have a clearer idea of what the therapy process is and what they hope to accomplish. The therapist in most instances has modified or confirmed his or her earlier formulations of what needs to be done and is set to monitor the application of his or her therapeutic plans. Certain features of the therapist's role and activities will essentially remain and continue throughout the remainder of therapy. The therapist should continue to manifest interest in the client, be an attentive and empathic listener, and reflect the client's feelings and concerns. At the same time, the therapist may increase the use of certain activities and procedures. For example, as the therapist gains greater understanding of the client and his or her difficulties, he or she is likely to offer more explanations and interpretations concerning the client's past and present adjustment. The therapist is also more likely to make use of other procedures and techniques such as providing information, role play, cognitive restructuring, relaxation, homework assignments, and any others that may be deemed useful.

The procedures and techniques used by the therapist in brief psychotherapy will depend on the therapist's theoretical orientation and the type of patient being seen. In the eclectic orientation that I follow, I emphasize the importance of the common therapeutic factors described in chapter 2, but I also make use of specific factors or techniques derived from any school of psychotherapy that empirically have been shown to have therapeutic efficacy. I also devote most attention to the patient's current situation, referring to some past events where they may elucidate the problem but not believing that the latter need particular emphasis. It is more important to change the patient's behavior, affect, or perceptions and beliefs about self and others than it is to ferret out possible psychodynamic causes or explanations of the patient's current problems.

Consequently, explanations or interpretations offered to the client tend to be based largely on the client's accounts of his or her current daily life interactions and on the therapist's observation of the client's behavior. For example, as a client relates her experiences with both her boss and her boyfriend, her subservient and passive pattern of interactions with important male figures becomes apparent. This pattern is also observable in how she relates to the male therapist. It may well be that her current problems in relating to men may stem from her earlier interactions with her father. However, knowing this may not necessarily change her behavior or improve her interpersonal problems. It seems more efficacious to point out her current pattern of relating to men, the consequences of her current behavior, and to plan some activities that may help her to change these patterns and improve her overall adjustment.

How these activities are handled by the therapist is also of some importance. The therapist must be especially sensitive to anything he or she says that might be interpreted as critical of the client or as being unsympathetic toward the client's problems. Thus, in pointing to self-defeating behavior patterns or to the specific behaviors displayed in the therapy session, the therapist must do so in a manner that simultaneously conveys sincere interest in the client, empathy, and a desire to help the client overcome his or her difficulties. In these interactions with the client, as with all interactions in psychotherapy, the therapist must be sincere and genuine. If the therapist is simply putting on an act or playing a role, it is doubtful if his or her interventions will be fully accepted by the client and thus lead to maximum improvement.

FOLLOWING THROUGH FROM THE EARLIER SESSIONS

As therapy proceeds, both client and therapist tend to feel more secure in their respective roles. Whatever initial doubts and concerns the client may have entertained about psychotherapy and the kind of person the therapist might be have generally subsided and have been replaced in most instances with a positive view of therapy and confidence in the therapist. As a result, most clients tend to feel freer and less constrained about confiding in the therapist and in revealing personal material. Problems and experiences that have produced some feelings of guilt or apprehension may be revealed during the early phases of the interim period. It is as if the client has to feel reasonably sure that the therapist can be trusted with such information and will also be understanding before it can be shared. Allowing and encouraging the client to bring up feelings, thoughts, and experiences that are troubling is an important aspect of therapy for a number of clients and may be extremely therapeutic for some.

Thus, as therapy continues, the client finds it easier to reveal more personal and intimate aspects of self. Also, if the therapist is able to respond in an empathic manner, the client is more likely to feel fully understood. These interacting aspects of psychotherapy, furthermore, strengthen the therapeutic relationship, facilitate the client's coopera-tion, and generally appear to move therapy along in a positive manner. Patient involvement becomes more clearly apparent and reinforces the efforts of both therapist and client.

During this phase of therapy, the client begins to apply some of the knowledge gained in the earlier sessions and to expand his or her understanding of self. Points made and brought up previously can be expanded, illustrated, questioned, and revised. Role plays may be used and homework assignments undertaken. Earlier formulations will be tested more adequately and new procedures tried over a longer period of time. In many respects, the middle or interim phase of psychotherapy is the largest component of therapy and perhaps the most important with respect to the amount of change that can be secured. Although a favorable start in the beginning sessions of psychotherapy does augur well for the remainder of psychotherapy, nothing is ever guaranteed, and future problems may arise as some issues are attacked more directly. For example, as mentioned earlier, the therapist may avoid further probing and questioning of the client in the early interviews. For a number of different reasons, such action may be avoided until the therapist believes he or she has a better understanding of the client's problem and more of a relationship has been developed.

Consequently, questions that may have been raised only in the therapist's mind initially may now be posed to the client. In a similar manner, observations noted in the early sessions may now be presented to the client and his or her reactions noted. Problem beliefs, perceptions, and behaviors may now be commented on by the therapist and the client confronted with their implications. In such instances, the therapist clearly is playing an active role in the therapy, and there are likely to be more active interchanges between the two participants than earlier in therapy.

A few illustrations may be helpful in showing how the therapist at this stage of therapy follows through on observations and formulations secured and developed in the preceding sessions. Consider the case of an individual who tends to keep his eyes averted during the sessions and never looks the therapist in the eye. Although the client does not mention this at all as a symptom when he discusses his lack of success both socially and vocationally, the therapist sees this as a behavioral pattern that may contribute to the client's difficulties. However, because commenting on this prematurely may be very embarrassing or disconcerting to the client, it is best for the therapist to note this pattern and to refrain from commenting on it or raising questions about it until the client is more familiar with the therapist and more secure in the therapy situation. At some point, however, the therapist will decide that it is worthwhile to comment on this behavior.

In commenting or drawing attention to any aspect of the client that may be perceived as negative, the therapist must be particularly alert to the impact of such comments on the client. As already emphasized, how such potentially provocative or critical statements are made is exceedingly important. If the behavior in question is one that the client may be particularly sensitive about or feel very inadequate about, it is especially important that the comment or question not be asked too soon—that is, before the client is able to face the problem with the support of the therapist. The therapist, therefore, must be a sensitive judge concerning the timing of such interventions. However, the therapist cannot postpone necessary interventions unnecessarily. It may be as poor a procedure to neglect an intervention or to overly delay an intervention as to intervene too soon. No precise guides can be offered the therapist on such matters. An accurate appraisal of the client is required, as well as a sound therapeutic relationship and skill in offering an interpretation, comment, or question in a manner that reflects the therapist's desire to help the client. These are not always easy to achieve, but they characterize the skilled therapist.

Therapists may also make note of unexplained gaps in the *accounts* provided by clients in the initial interview. If there is no overriding reason to probe such items during this initial interview, the matter can be returned to at a later session when it appears pertinent. For example, a client discussing past events may mention dropping out of college, breaking up with a girlfriend, or having been married twice before and provide relatively few details. Such items may need to be explored in greater detail in order to help clarify certain patterns of behavior that lead to failure and related negative consequences or to allow the client to give full expression to troublesome feelings that are bottled up. If a client tells the therapist that he or she "flunked out" of college and there are no accompanying cues to indicate anything unusual in this account, little or no explanation may be required. On the other hand, if a client states that he or she dropped out after 2 years of college and very quickly goes on to discuss something else or gives a rather evasive answer, this item may be of potential significance. If the client does not bring this matter up voluntarily a few interviews later, the therapist should consider carefully the possible reasons for this and decide when it might be appropriate to do so. Individuals drop out of school for many different reasons, and some of them are mentioned with no hesitation whatsoever. However, such reasons as cheating, stealing in the dorm, sexual assault, and being pregnant may not be as readily forthcoming from clients and yet may have considerable significance for the client's current adjustment.

The preceding comments should not be interpreted as indicating that the therapist needs to explore every item of a detailed personal history that could not be sketched out in sufficient detail in the initial interview. As already mentioned, there is no need for an overly detailed life history, and the therapist should focus on topics pertaining to the client's presenting problems and current life situation. I refer to items of potential significance that the client seems to avoid or skip over and that he or she may not be ready to discuss or divulge until a later stage of therapy. Such items, of course, may not be as important as they seemed, and important new material not previously mentioned may be brought up by the client in subsequent interviews. The therapist thus tries to follow through on material mentioned in the very early sessions and is also ready to deal with new information and new problems as they arise.

POTENTIAL THERAPEUTIC PROBLEMS

Even when all seems to start well in therapy, things may change and problems may arise from time to time. This is one reason, among others, that the psychotherapist must be flexible in his or her approach and adapt matters to meet changing situations. At any time in therapy, something may happen in a client's life that is of great importance to him or her and overrides other concerns including matters pertaining to therapy. Clearly, the therapist must devote attention to such developments and their obvious impact on the client. A discussion of some of the types of problems that may arise during therapy is presented in this section.

We have already discussed in some detail the problem of missing and cancelling appointments, and our discussion here can be very brief. As is true with such matters in the early therapy sessions, they need to be clarified with the client. If no truly adequate reason is provided by the client, this behavior needs to be viewed as a problem, and the therapist must attempt to understand the reasons for it. In a general way, missed appointments may be viewed as a sign of less than satisfactory progress. If the therapist can discover what may be at fault and is able to change the situation accordingly, the problem may be resolved. If this is not possible, then the therapist most likely will have to discuss the issue with the client and try to find out what the cause might be. The therapist can try to deal with the problem in a nonaccusatory way. For example, he or she can say something like the following: "In the past few weeks, as you know, you have missed a couple of appointments, and I have wondered if perhaps something about the therapy is bothering you or upsetting you in some way so that you find yourself wanting not to come to therapy. Your own feelings about therapy are important."

If the client does respond to this type of inquiry, the matter can be discussed and the issue resolved. If the client resists acknowledging that anything is wrong and insists on keeping to reasons that do not appear adequate (e.g., forgot, was involved in an activity, didn't have my watch), the situation becomes more difficult and there are no ready solutions. I tend to interpret this type of pattern as a lack of patient involvement or poor therapeutic handling on my part and feel that the prognosis is not good. If this happens in the relatively early sessions (fourth through seventh), I consider the possibility of premature termination likely. If it occurs at later sessions, it may indicate a desire on the part of the client to conclude therapy, either because an impasse has been reached in therapy or because the client has secured what he or she sought from therapy.

All such behaviors on the part of the client are a form of communication to the therapist. They show that the client is not carrying out his or her prescribed or expected role in psychotherapy. Consequently, the therapist cannot afford to overlook this behavioral message and must attempt to respond in order to discover what lies behind this behavior. In the case of missed appointments at relatively late sessions (e.g., after seven sessions or so), the therapist sould consider the possibility that the client has achieved sufficient help from therapy but may not be able to express clearly that additional therapy is really not required. For a variety of reasons, psychotherapists may be reluctant to terminate clients, particularly clients who have participated well in therapy and are well regarded by the therapist. The topic of termination is discussed in greater detail in a subsequent chapter, but it is worth mentioning here to emphasize that issues concerning termination may come up at any stage of therapy. If a client has shown progress and previously has kept regular appointments, a missed appointment should be evaluated as objectively as possible by the therapist. The possibility that the client feels enough has been accomplished in therapy must be considered seriously by the therapist, and if this seems plausible, a discussion of possible termination should occur.

Another type of problem that may arise occasionally is a change in the rate of progess as therapy continues. Psychotherapy rarely seems to follow a straight line progression with equal increments of improvement each week. On the basis of a moderate amount of research, it appears that the most important activities, including degree of change, occur during the first eight sessions (Garfield, 1986; Howard et al., 1986). By the eighth session, approximately half of the patients have shown improvement, and over half who began therapy have already terminated in one fashion or another. At the same time, however, a significant number have not progressed in a comparable fashion and are still engaged in therapy. Consequently, a variety of patterns of patient change and concurrent views of the therapeutic process may be anticipated.

In some instances, clients may exhibit considerable interest and enthusiasm at the beginning of therapy, and then this degree of enthusiasm may wane after a few sessions. Conceivably, this may be due to overinflated expectations about how quickly changes will occur as a result of psychotherapy, to some error or mishandling of the case on the part of the therapist, to misperceptions on the client's part as to what is occurring, or to some events that have occurred outside of the clinical situation. When the therapist observes such a pattern, he or she should strive to ascertain what factors may be responsible for it. Because some clients may be reticent about volunteering information that can be viewed as critical of the therapist or as illustrating additional ineptness on the client's part, the therapist can at least wonder out loud as to whether something has happened recently to cause some change in the client's behavior—for example, "I wonder if something has happened recently. You seem somewhat down in the mouth and less spirited than usual." If the client seems reluctant to provide much information, the therapist can make some reference either to possible events in the client's life, if this seems likely, or to the client's possible concerns dealing more directly with therapy or the therapist—for example, "Have some new problems come up with regard to your son?" "Has something occurred in the last few sessions that has been upsetting to you?"

In such interactions, the therapist can try to ascertain what may be causing the change in the client's behavior. However, unless there is an unusually marked impasse in therapy that may be viewed as a possible indication of serious deterioration in the therapeutic relationship, the therapist, in most instances, should not be overly aggressive in questioning the client. There should be no formal interrogation. Rather, the therapist's questions should be raised in a manner that conveys his or her sensitivity to the client's feelings and sincere interest in wanting to help the client. If the client seems reluctant to become engaged in responding to the therapist's inquiry, the therapist can simply note this and turn to other matters of present concern.

Although some clients may be reluctant to openly discuss dissatisfactions or problems with therapy, there are other clients who do not exhibit such reticence or inhibition, and a few references to such clients were made in earlier chapters. No therapist likes to be criticized or to receive negative feedback from clients, but all therapists should be prepared to receive such responses from some clients at some time. It is also difficult to remain calm and objective at all times, although the therapist has a professional obligation to strive to do so. However, critical comments or even seemingly innocent questions from clients are important communications and for the most part may signify the existence of some kind of problem in therapy. Such comments and questions also reflect the personality of the client, and although they may be related to the problems for which the client seeks therapy, they must also be viewed and responded to as current problems in therapy—

problems that need to be overcome in order for therapy to progress in a successful manner. The therapist must be able to respond in a manner that focuses on the current therapy issue in order not to be viewed by the client as retaliating against the client's criticism by pointing to the personal deficiencies of the client.

Potentially critical comments or questions, consequently, must be explored carefully with the client. Ostensibly, the task here is not having to find out that the client is dissatisfied in some way with therapy, but to discover what the problems are and how to deal with them. For example, I have had some clients who stated that therapy didn't seem to be helping them or solving their problems, and occasionally a client has simply inquired how many more sessions will be required before they get better. In both of these instances, it seems clear that the therapist must allow the client to verbalize his or her dissatisfaction and concerns. If such concerns reflect mainly a misunderstanding on the part of the client, the matter can be resolved quite easily by clarifying the misunderstanding. In some instances, the question raised by the client may actually be a sincere request for information and not one that is loaded with psychodynamic implications. Thus, the query as to how many more sessions would be required for improvement to take place was asked by a man who was considering a new position in another city, and it did have relevance concerning a possible date for the move.

In the more difficult cases where such a question or critical comment seems likely to be a reflection of the client's interpersonal problems, the therapist must proceed slowly and cautiously in exploring the issue with the client. I would first reflect back the client's feelings of disappointment at the apparent lack of progress and allow him or her to release negative feelings and elaborate on his or her statement in any way. Depending on the specific client, I might empathize with his or her feelings that therapy is progressing slower than desired and ask what the client had hoped would be accomplished by this time (e.g., the fourth or fifth interview). If the client was not overly disappointed and primarily was seeking reassurance from the therapist, this could be handled in a reasonably matter of fact way. The client can be told that therapy is still in a relatively early stage and that the situation can be reappraised at some time in the future. In this instance, a specific number of sessions can be mentioned—for example, three, four, or five sessions. Also, if the client seems to seek reassurance and encouragement beyond what would be considered reasonable, this can be noted by the therapist and discussed as part of the client's problems at a later time.

Where the client is clearly more critical of the therapy or of the therapist than was evident in the previous cases or than seems justified, resolution of the problem is both more difficult and more complicated. First of all, the therapist must keep his or her own feelings under control and evaluate very quickly if there is some merit to the client's complaint. If there is, then the therapist must acknowledge this and attempt to give some explanation as to what may have occurred. For example, the therapist may have been overly optimistic in predicting rate of improvement, or the client may have misinterpreted what was said in the initial interview. If such discussion seems to clarify matters sufficiently, therapy can proceed, although the therapist should be alerted to the possibility of future occurrences of this type. However, if it seems apparent that the client is expressing criticism of therapy that is quite hostile in tone, and there have been a few hints of such behavior in the earlier sessions, then the therapist must deal with the client's critical behavior as an important part of the client's current difficulties outside of therapy. Such an interpretation of the client's behavior does constitute a real confrontation with the client but is necessary if any potential progress is to be secured in therapy. It is better, in my opinion, to try to resolve this problem than to let it linger without resolution or to avoid it altogether. Future negative interactions can be anticipated, and these most likely will not be very therapeutic. A possible attempt to deal with this type of problem is described in the following excerpt.

> *Client (C):* "I've been wondering when this therapy is supposed to start working. Thus far I come to these sessions and nothing seems to be happening."
>
> *Therapist (T):* "You're disappointed that progress seems to be much slower than you had anticipated—is that it?"
>
> *C:* "Yeah. All we seem to do is talk, and I do most of the talking. I don't see where this gets us anywhere."
>
> *T:* "Perhaps it might be worthwhile to clarify what you thought might be taking place in therapy."
>
> *C:* "Well, I thought you would be helping me improve my . . . helping me to get along better—and you really haven't done much and I still feel the same way."
>
> *T:* "So, you're saying that I haven't performed as you expected—is that it?"
>
> *C:* "Yeah—that's right."
>
> *T:* "What was it that you were expecting me to do?"
>
> *C:* "Well, you could be telling me why other people get the breaks and I don't, or why I seem to be the fall guy all the time."
>
> *T:* "From what you're saying it seems as if you're angry because therapy hasn't gone the way you wanted it to and I haven't played the role you would have liked me to play."
>
> *C:* "Yeah. I guess that's about it."
>
> *T:* "Alright, let's explore this situation. You expected or wanted me to conduct therapy in a way that you would have preferred, but not necessarily in the way that I described to you earlier. In other words, I didn't behave or function as you would have liked me to, and as a result

of this, you became angry at me. Now, I wonder if something like this also happens outside."

C: "What do you mean?"

T: "What I'm suggesting is that what has taken place here in terms of the two of us may actually be what occurs in your relation to other people. If you would like or expect people to react toward you in a certain way, and they don't react that way, it irritates you and makes you angry—as I believe has happened here. And, when people sense this irritation and anger in you, they try to avoid interacting with you.

C: (Pause). "Well, that could happen sometimes—some people are overly sensitive and you can't please everybody, but I don't know that that explains everything.

T: "That's true, but don't you think it's worth examining and trying to understand? If what I say may have some validity, we may be able to focus on something of importance."

In the preceding hypothetical case I have tried to illustrate one possible type of therapist response to a potential problem arising during therapy. In this illustration, the client makes some statements that are quite critical of the psychotherapy in process, and the therapist responds by reflecting what he perceives as the client's underlying feelings. This leads to the matter of the client's wishes or expectations being unfilled (although not based on inputs from the therapist) and resulting in irritation and anger that is communicated to others. The therapist goes on to relate this pattern of behavior to some of the difficulties experienced by the client. This transition to a discussion of the client's actual problems is a very positive one if it can be achieved. In real life, this type of quick transition may not always work, and in some instances the therapist may be viewed antagonistically as defensive and critical of the client. When this occurs, the problem becomes more difficult and the client is liable to drop out of therapy. However, nothing is really gained by ignoring such problems, for in such cases clients also may decide to terminate their therapy.

Before concluding this section, I mention the impact of some crisis or other significant event in the patient's life on what occurs in psychotherapy. Although the therapist may have a specific treatment plan as a guide and framework for the psychotherapy he or she is conducting, when some kind of crisis or tragedy occurs in the patient's life, the crisis must take precedence and become the immediate focus of therapy. A physical injury, loss of a loved one, a divorce threat, and a loss of a job are all such potentially devastating experiences that they deserve the primary attention of the therapist. Sometimes such crises can be handled over a few interviews by allowing the patient to express his or her feelings, by supportive reassurance, and by facilitating plans for coping with the present situation. When these are resolved successfully, attention can be devoted to other matters.

EVALUATING PROGRESS AND PROCEDURES

It is both a wise and necessary therapeutic rule to try to evaluate how therapy is proceeding and whether or not actual progress is being made. Besides the fact that the original assessment of the client and his or her problem may undergo change and have to be modified, there is also the likelihood that the formulations and plans for therapy will also have to undergo change. Actually, we already have anticipated this eventuality in our previous discussion of potential problems in psychotherapy. When the therapist becomes aware of a problem in therapy, he or she actually has engaged in some type of evaluation process. However, the evaluative process should go on throughout therapy even when no serious problem is anticipated or encountered. This is necessitated in great part because of the very nature of psychotherapy, which requires an adaptation to the individual case, and also because of an ethical requirement to do the best in the shortest possible time and to avoid harming the client in any way.

Progress in psychotherapy, as noted, does not occur necessarily at a regular and uniform rate. Consequently, the therapist must check his or her observations of what is occurring in psychotherapy and not reach conclusions prematurely. I recall listening to a presentation at a professional meeting many years ago that made a very strong impression on me. A well-known behavior therapist reported on his work with a mentally retarded child who essentially had no speech. This psychologist used an operant conditioning approach and rewarded the child with candy and praise whenever she verbalized any sound. A large number of learning trials were conducted with very little meaningful progress, and then some verbalizations were made and a rapid improvement took place. I remember thinking to myself that I would have given up long before any positive change was evident, and I admired this therapist for his knowledge as well as persistence. (He also kept a meticulous record of all his interactions with the child.)

I do not want to give the reader the impression that the therapist should persevere and continue with therapy despite evidence of no progress. On the contrary, I strongly disapprove of unnecessarily prolonging the length of psychotherapy, and that is one reason for the need to evaluate the client's progress during psychotherapy. However, it is important to have some reasonably valid expectations about what can be accomplished within certain time frames and to be concerned if there is a clear lack of progress. For example, if the therapist is seeing a client who meets the general criteria of being a suitable candidate for brief psychotherapy and there is no discernible progress after five or six interviews, the therapist should attempt some evaluation of the case.

This would include a reappraisal of the client, his or her current complaints, the general formulation of the case, the procedures used, and the therapist's feelings about the case. Such a reappraisal may give the therapist some possible clues as to what may be responsible for the lack of progress or as to what procedures need to be modified.

In some cases of lack of progress, it may be desirable to discuss the issue with the client to see if there is a possible explanation for it. Although not likely, there are instances where important problems occur in the client's life that have not been the focus of therapy and have not been mentioned by the client. It is also possible that the client has not been attempting to follow through on some of the suggestions or homework assignments offered by the therapist. In discussing the apparent lack of progress, the therapist also has an opportunity to evaluate more adequately the client's attitude toward therapy and the therapist.

Depending on the evaluations of the therapist and the information secured from the client, the therapist can try to make certain accommodations in his or her therapeutic activities. In some cases, the changes deemed desirable can be made with very little difficulty; in others, the possibility for effecting the necessary changes may be more difficult. Sometimes the therapist initially may not be as perceptive of the specific sensitivities of a given client and thus needs to proceed more slowly than previously planned. A certain rigidity in the personality of the client may become much clearer at a later point in therapy and may have to be dealt with before real progress can be made.

In a previous discussion of a case in which the client failed to bring in her record of what she had eaten and the time and circumstances of these occurrences, an evaluation was made by the therapist of the significance of this behavior. This pattern could be viewed as resistive and noncollaborative behavior on the part of the client—I'm confident that at least some therapists would view it in this way. However, in this particular instance, the therapist, perhaps intuitively, decided not to make a real issue of the forgetfulness of the client. The problem of being overweight was not seen as the most important of the client's problems, and consequently the therapist decided to pass over the matter somewhat lightly and deal with other matters. The forgetful behavior was not neglected or overlooked. Instead, the evaluation made by the therapist led to a judgment that other matters were more important. Also, the client gave other indications of collaborating with the therapist and being involved in therapy and this, too, entered into the therapist's decision. Thus, various features of the case were evaluated and a decision was reached by the therapist to focus on certain ones and to give less attention to others.

Because of the variability in patient personality as well as symptomatology, the therapist cannot necessarily expect all patients to improve at the same rate. All the therapist can do is to use his or her knowledge and experience to evaluate the progress or lack of progress in therapy with the individual patient. There are some cases, however, where a lack of adequate progress may be somewhat easier to identify. One group of cases in this category are mild to moderately depressed individuals. With interpersonal, behavioral, or cognitive approaches, research studies indicate that a majority of patients will respond positively to relatively brief psychotherapy (Lewinsohn & Hoberman, 1982; Rush, Beck, Kovacs, & Hollon, 1977; Weissman et al., 1979). This has also been my experience with a more eclectic approach. Consequently, if there is no clearly visible improvement after eight or so therapy sessions, the therapist should re-evaluate the situation and see what possible factors may be involved. Consulting authoritative reference works on depression may be helpful in this regard (e.g., Beck, 1976; Paykel, 1982). If there does not appear to be any adequate explanation for the lack of progress, the therapist should monitor the following sessions carefully to see if there are any aspects that may have been missed. If this pattern continues, the therapist might consider some type of consultation or referral. It is always a difficult decision to decide when it is best to make a referral or to continue with the patient in therapy when therapeutic progress is very slow. The therapist doesn't want to abandon a patient unnecessarily, and termination or referral may be viewed in this fashion by the client or the therapist. On the other hand, keeping a patient in therapy when there is no indication of any meaningful progress and no indication that such progress is forthcoming is not a professionally desirable practice.

Other types of cases that generally can be expected to respond positively to brief psychotherapy are those with situational anxiety reactions, cases with specific current crises, acute grief reactions, and similar types of problems. Anxiety reactions, in most cases, will respond to an approach utilizing desensitization, emotional release, and empathic understanding and encouragement from the therapist. Where specific phobias are concerned, exposure treatment appears to be the treatment of choice (Mathews et al., 1981; O'Leary & Wilson, 1987). When cases such as these do not respond with some progress after a reasonable period of time, the therapist should re-evaluate the case and attempt to discover what factors may be responsible for the situation. Is the nature of the problem more severe than it had appeared earlier? Are there errors or limitations in the way the case is being treated? Have external events had a negative impact on therapeutic progress? Are there related problems that seem to be inhibiting or complicating the previous therapeutic work?

I recall one case seen in a university training clinic that, although not typical, may illustrate at least in part some of the points made in the preceding section. The client was a divorced woman in her mid-thirties who came to the clinic for help with her driving phobia. Although she appeared somewhat "flighty," she clearly indicated that she was only concerned with getting over her phobia and being able to drive again. In fact, at the time, she appeared to be the closest thing to a textbook case for systematic desensitization. The student-therapist assigned to the case was also quite interested in behavior therapy and relied mainly on systematic desensitization in working with this woman. At the end of the therapy, which consisted of about 15 sessions, the client had shown real progress, although she was not completely rid of her phobia. She could drive in the neighborhood and could drive to a busy shopping area if someone was with her in the car. The client resumed her therapy with a new therapist when the new academic year began, and a number of events occurred that seemed to have quite an adverse effect on the client. The new therapist did not have as positive a view of the client as the previous one and was unable to develop a truly effective relationship. Of even greater significance were events occurring at that time in the client's life. She was having difficulties with her father (she and her daughter lived with her parents), and then while accompanying some friends in their car, the car was hit by another car and the client suffered serious physical injury. The latter events pushed the driving phobia somewhat into the background, and with the emergence of other symptoms, including depression, the therapeutic plan had to be significantly modified with a greater emphasis on empathic listening, emotional release, and cognitive restructuring.

Perhaps enough has been said concerning the need to evaluate the client's progress during the interim phase of psychotherapy. I do not intend to increase unnecessarily the anxiety or morbid introspection of the therapist. Rather, my purpose has been to highlight this one aspect of the therapist's role and responsibility. Both on the basis of research findings and clinical experience, it is evident that not every patient who receives psychotherapy manifests significant improvement at the end of therapy. This is not a reason for despair, but rather a facing of the reality of professional practice—at least for the present. On the positive side, psychotherapists do provide a large number of distressed individuals with therapeutic help. However, it is important for the psychotherapist to evaluate his or her work as therapy proceeds, and when progress appears limited he or she must consider possible alternatives and modifications. The therapist can decide to respond differently, add a new procedure, allow more time for observation and appraisal, seek a consultation, terminate therapy, or refer the patient elsewhere. There are thus a number of alternatives or actions that the therapist can take after considered deliberation and evaluation.

THE CONTINUING THERAPY
PROCESS

As has been indicated, the therapist must always evaluate what he or she is doing and how the client is responding. On this basis, the therapist may decide to continue or modify his or her approach to the particular client and also to make use of additional techniques and procedures. Sometimes changes result from additional information provided by the client; sometimes it seems appropriate to move from verbal expression and interaction to more behavioral activities, such as role play; and at other times adding new components to therapy actually may have been part of the early therapeutic plan.

The therapist is in charge of the therapeutic work and has the responsibility to see that therapy proceeds as effectively and efficiently as possible. This is especially true in the practice of brief psychotherapy. Consequently, the role of the therapist demands appraisal, activity, and flexibility. The therapist cannot sit back passively and wait for the client to bring forth the important insights and changes.

Although there are apparently several hundred different schools of psychotherapy, the number of possible therapeutic techniques and procedures are considerably less. This is certainly an interesting phenomenon and may explain at least partially why some authors have attempted to combine many of the approaches into just a few categories, such as psychodynamic, behavioral, cognitive, and humanistic (Beutler, 1983; Glad, 1959; Howard, Nance, & Myers, 1987; Schofield, 1988). Although each of the various approaches to psychotherapy claim to be what I have termed *universal therapies*, good for all types of disorders, at least a number of individuals in the field view them as effective primarily for certain types of disorders or for certain types of individuals. The idea is that the founders of each school developed their theories and procedures mainly by working with a particular type of clientele. Consequently, the effective therapist needs to know about three or four major approaches, and then he or she can select from among them the one deemed most appropriate for specific patients with particular problems (Schofield, 1988).

Although this type of view certainly is appealing, I believe it is overly simplistic and does not really fit with the overall data on outcome in psychotherapy. As I emphasized earlier, there are many common factors among the different approaches and also some specific techniques that are particularly effective for specific types of problems. Although the different forms of psychotherapy can be ranked on certain dimensions such as degree of structures, therapist directiveness, or emphasis on reflection of feelings, these represent formal descriptive features of the therapies. They do not include potential common factors that are usually omitted in the formal descriptions of the therapies, nor do they indicate the actual range of behaviors that therapists display in their therapeutic work. Thus, they are really incomplete and overly abstract characterizations of all the interactions that actually occur when therapists of a given orientation perform their therapeutic work. Also, with a few exceptions, there is no clear-cut evidence that one form of psychotherapy is unequivocally superior to others in the treatment of specific disorders (Lambert et al., 1986).

Despite theoretical differences, therefore, there are many commonalities among the various psychotherapies, and the number of different techniques and procedures available to therapists is comparatively limited. For example, practically all approaches to psychotherapy attempt to secure some type of cognitive or perceptual modification. In some approaches, the major theoretical emphasis is on changing cognitions, and thus we expect such an emphasis in these approaches to psychotherapy. In rational emotive therapy, Ellis (1962) clearly stressed the basic importance of changing irrational beliefs—but he did a lot of other things in therapy as well. Beck (1976) called his approach to therapy cognitive therapy, and in his work with depressed patients attempted to get them to change their view of themselves, their situation, and the future—but a number of other things are involved as well. A number of cognitive-behavior therapists also devote attention to the cognitions of their clients, although they may indicate stronger allegiance to formal theories of learning. Psychodynamic therapists also try to change the perceptions and beliefs of their clients, but their approach and the kinds of cognitive changes they emphasize may differ noticeably from those of the others.

Thus, a large number of therapeutic approaches focus on cognitions and cognitive change, and in many instances there is considerable similarity in what is emphasized in this area. Faulty perceptions and beliefs, overly self-critical attitudes, and the like are recognized by most therapists as problems that need to be modified in a more positive direction. Although the theories and the terminology may differ, the objectives and the actual process of change likely have much in common. In this process, the therapist attempts to help the client see that his or her perceptions or cognitions are unrealistic or distorted and points out how they contribute to the client's difficulties.

As therapy continues, the therapist may also develop a better understanding of the kinds of preoccupations and negative self-talk that occupy the client and contribute to feelings of insecurity and apprehension. As a result, there may be a gradual reduction in the therapist's general use of reflection of feeling and a more concentrated focus on and discussion of these cognitions and expectancies. In such explorations with the client, the therapist can note associations and connections between the unverbalized thoughts of the client and affects and behaviors that appear to be derived from or associated with these thoughts. It is important to point out such relationships to the client as the first step in attempting to change such patterns and their negative consequences.

In this connection, it is worth emphasizing that in psychotherapy the therapist always deals with the patient's perceptions of self and environment. These perceptions may not necessarily correspond to how others view the same set of stimuli. Actually, the patient's view may differ considerably from the views of others without necessarily constituting serious pathology. However, to the extent that these perceptions and associated beliefs are distorted or faulty and contribute to the patient's discomfort, some attempts must be made to change them.

A few years ago on a professional visit, I was asked to interview a young woman who was receiving psychotherapy at an outpatient clinic of a medical school. On the basis of the description of the patient and the therapy summary presented by the patient's therapist, it was quite evident that the patient had a self-deprecating view of herself and that she was concerned about her general appearance. When she arrived for my interview, she made a much more positive impression on me than I had anticipated. Actually, she was an attractive young woman who had convinced herself that she really was unattractive. During the interview, I asked her in a direct manner how she had reached this faulty view of herself. It seemed that at a younger age she had been chubby and had felt herself to be unattractive in comparison with her sister. I readily acknowledged that she might have been less attractive when she was younger, but asked her what that had to do with her appearance now. In the interview, besides telling her that I thought she was an attractive young lady, I was able to point out that she was telling herself something that was not true but was believing it and acting on it as if it were true, to her own discomfort. This seemed to have some impact on her and appeared to be reinforced by the fact that while we were talking I mirrored her bodily stance and those movements that had seemed to me to reflect her non-positive view of self. I did so with a smile on my face to illustrate what we had been discussing, and she appeared to smile knowingly in response. By this behavior I was not being critical of her but was actually empathizing with her feelings, and her response seemed to indicate that she understood.

In this case, the interview was not a regular therapy interview but a consultative demonstration interview conducted for the outpatient staff. Nevertheless, a good relationship with the client was established, there was real interaction between the two of us, and I was able to bring into focus some aspects of the individual's problems that had not received sufficient attention previously. The discussion about the distorted self-view plus my verbalized positive evaluation of the young woman represented some emphases that had not been made by the regular therapist previously. However, the therapist did feel that these were important aspects and would be responded to in the future sessions. Of course, that I was a so-called visiting expert may have tilted the scales in my favor.

Reference can also be made to the case of a young man who complained of being unable to communicate easily with others in social situations. He stated that he felt he had difficulty in saying anything that was of interest to others. According to him, he could only speak of very superficial topics. Consequently, he would tend to get somewhat tongue-tied and very uncomfortable when he had to call someone or had to engage in social conversation. This was particularly true in interactions with women. It was evident that this person's view of his verbal inadequacy led to some implicit self-verbalization when he was in certain social situations or was on a date with a female friend. His inner communications or cognitions were somewhat along the following lines: "All I can say or talk about are inconsequential trivia. This person is going to think I'm stupid. Oh, I wish I would think of something worthwhile to say. I wonder what she thinks of me. I think she must be bored."

All of this inner communication and self-preoccupation has a very self-critical tone. It occurs in the social situation and actually increases the individual's anxiety and concern. It thus acts as a barrier to effective social interaction, increases the individual's lack of confidence and negative self-view, and tends to decrease attempts at future interactions. In this particular case, when I suggested to the client what I thought went through his mind in these situations, he replied strongly in the affirmative and then gave examples similar to the foregoing.

It is evident from such examples that there is an interaction between perceptions, cognitions, affect, and behavior. The perception or belief of self-inadequacy leads to internal communication about the expected negative response or evaluation from others. This, in turn, appears to lead to an increase in anxiety and discomfort, which in turn lessens approach behaviors and increases avoidant behaviors. Consequently, in therapy it is desirable to try an approach that can impact on all related components, if this is at all possible.

In the aforementioned case, such an approach was attempted with some success. After the client had been given the opportunity to discuss his thoughts and feelings about his inadequacies in communicating with others in social situations, I pointed out and discussed with him a number of important aspects that had seemingly coalesced into a regular pattern. Even before entering any kind of social interaction, he set up expectations of being responded to as inadequate because he would not be able to think of anything worthwhile to say. In other words, he predicted dire consequences and was set to view the responses of others in this way. Because of this predisposition, he was unable actually to validate his perceptions and experience in a realistic manner. In essence, he was inclined to see what he expected to see.

A couple of sessions were devoted to clarifying these patterns so the client could understand and appreciate how they influenced his feelings and behavior. An attempt was also made to encourage him to try and change his perceptions and thoughts in order to make them more congruent with the actual social reality. Although he believed people were negatively inclined toward him because of his social limitations, he actually could not make a strong case to support this belief. I was able to use his own descriptions to point out how his conclusions were highly colored by his expectations and beliefs. For example, if he went out with someone and that person did not phone him within a few days, he felt it was due to his inadequate conversational abilities, even though there was actually no basis for such an expectation. As a result of these discussions, he somewhat reluctantly began to see the reality of what I was attempting to point out to him. This was a necessary first step but just the initial part of this particular process.

Although this client could accept the part his expectations and cognitions played in the maintenance of his difficulties, this was not sufficient to reduce his discomfort or to make him feel more adequate in his social interactions. In order to try to attain these goals, I became somewhat more directive and made use of some cognitive-behavioral techniques. Because he had readily agreed that he silently verbalized negative and self-defeating thoughts, I suggested that he now try to verbalize more positive and realistic thoughts. I also stated that although this sounded like a rather superficial suggestion, it was worth a try if he agreed. When he agreed, I went on to offer some other procedures that I thought might be helpful to him. I told him I was going to give him some homework to do, and that although many people don't like to do homework, some of it is very worthwhile. This was done in a semi-humorous manner, smiling, and he responded in a comparable manner. Specifically, I asked him to make some telephone calls and arrange for some social activities. He was anxious about making such calls. I also suggested that he could think in advance about things he could talk about with the parties involved. These procedures were followed for the next few weeks and had a positive impact. The client admitted that my assigning homework tasks to him definitely helped him to perform these tasks. Because he also admitted that he was still a bit anxious prior to making these calls, I also gave him some brief instructions on relaxation procedures. The idea here was that he could relax himself prior to the phone calls and use relaxation as a coping mechanism (Goldfried & Trier, 1974).

The suggestions and procedures used with this individual were directly related to the problems for which he sought therapy. Their potential use became apparent as I was able to make an adequate appraisal of the client on the basis of the first few interviews. I felt more confident about the client, about the therapeutic procedures that could be used, and about the possibility of a favorable outcome. Of definite importance was the development of a very positive, mutually-respectful relationship between the client and me. Thus, homework assignments and related suggestions were not seen as artificial or trivial tasks but as procedures that reflected my sincere interest in wanting to help the client.

As the problems of the client become better understood and as a good working relationship with the client becomes established, the therapist's confidence in what needs to be done is also heightened. The therapist feels freer to offer suggestions, to provide homework assignments, and even to confront the client on matters of importance. He or she is better able to clarify or modify therapeutic goals and to select new procedures when they seem to be of potential use. At the same time, the therapist must be aware that therapy does not always proceed on a smooth and upward path. Also, despite the therapist's best efforts at assessing and working with clients, from time to time he or she may encounter an occasional crisis with some client. Although such events may be rare, they have a strong impact on the therapist and require considerable judgment and fortitude. Consequently, a brief discussion of possible problems of this type follows.

POTENTIAL CRISES

Although the therapist is responsible for devising a plan for therapy, for selecting the procedures and techniques to be used, and for monitoring the progress of therapy, he or she cannot control completely the process of psychotherapy. The client obviously also plays a very significant role in what goes on in therapy. The client's problems or pathology, personality, social support system, and unexpected events occurring in the client's life all may affect the process of therapy. Although, as compared with long-term psychotherapy, crises in brief psychotherapy are undoubtedly less frequent, some may occur. When a crisis does occur, it places additional stress on the therapist and may also call for some modification in the current therapeutic activities. In some cases, the crisis may be indirectly related to some lack of sensitivity or ineptness on the part of the therapist. In other cases, it may be due to some significant and upsetting incidents occurring in the client's life.

When the progress in psychotherapy suddenly appears to be reversed and when the client's clinical condition appears to be seriously worsened, the therapist faces some type of crisis in therapy. At such a point, the psychotherapist must evaluate the possible factors accounting for this negative turn and decide on what steps need to be taken to alleviate the trouble. One such crisis is sometimes encountered when a patient becomes acutely depressed and verbalizes suicidal thoughts. The therapist must gauge the severity of the suicidal ideation and not overreact. There is little question that the client's threat of suicide is one of the most disturbing events that can occur during psychotherapy. During such a period the therapist must try to get the patient to verbalize his or her feelings of hopelessness and challenge his or her self-defeating cognitions. Depending on the case, it may also be desirable to increase the frequency of the therapy sessions until the acute period passes. If the depression and suicidal thoughts are judged to be very severe, it may be wise to refer the patient for a psychiatric consultation and possible antidepressant medication.

Crises and difficult challenges of this type require skill, wisdom, and considerable emotional strength and maturity on the part of the therapist. Important decisions must be made in a timely way. In some instances, perhaps, it may be necessary to have a patient hospitalized. On the other hand, unnecessarily hospitalizing a patient may have a nontherapeutic effect on the patient, because it indicates a lack of confidence in the psychological strength and coping skills of the patient. Thus, the therapist must be sure that the decision is based on his or her objective clinical appraisal and not on his or her own level of anxiety. In my own clinical experience, I have been fortunate in not having to hospitalize a patient. This may be because psychotherapy has usually been a part-time activity for me. However, I recall a few cases that did cause me some concern. In the case of a mildly depressed young man who became very deeply depressed as a result of a change in his professional situation, I referred him to a psychiatric colleague of mine, who prescribed an antidepressant medication for him. I also increased the frequency of our visits to twice a week instead of once a week. After two weeks, this severe episode diminished and the patient was able to resume a more normal pattern of activities. However, this period, relatively brief though it was, represented a real crisis for both therapist and patient.

In another case where depression was also a prominent symptom, I made a somewhat different decision. The client could be described as a hysterical personality with depression. At one fairly early session, she came in with very negative verbalizations and also cried through most of the session. Although I was concerned about the strong feelings of discomfort and pain experienced by this patient and tried to respond empathically, I did not feel that there was any serious danger of suicide and believed that her mood would not continue at this level for any long period. As it turned out, this was a pattern she displayed from time to time, and its intensity did diminish.

Obviously, the more accurate the therapist's appraisal and understanding of the client, the better able he or she is to evaluate the impact of the crisis on the client's stability and ability to cope. The formal clinical diagnosis of the client tells the therapist something about the client, but by itself it is insufficient. The therapist also needs to be aware of the degree of the client's pathology, the client's personality strengths and weaknesses, the client's current life situation, and the existing therapeutic relationship. Serious deficiencies in any of these areas are potential sources of concern and need to be evaluated very carefully. Unfortunately, there is no statistical formula that can be offered to guide the therapist in making such appraisals. Clinical acumen and experience are the therapist's main guides until adequate research data on such problems are secured.

In the past, therapists seemingly were most concerned about potential client suicide and also about possible assaultive behavior directed against them by hostile, aggressive clients with poor controls. Both concerns are easily understandable. In the case of hostile and aggressive clients, it is clear that accurate assessment of the client and his or her potential for acting out behavior is of primary importance. The therapist, therefore, must decide whether or not the client can profit from psychotherapy and whether he or she is willing to accept the client for individual psychotherapy. Thus, there are really two decisions that therapists must make: Is this client a suitable candidate for psychotherapy? Do I want to be the therapist? In most instances, the answer to the two questions will be the same, but they do not necessarily have to be the same.

In a recent study of the sources of stress among psychotherapists, the two that were ranked most frequently were suicidal statements made by the client and the therapist's inability to help an acutely distressed client to feel better (Deutsch, 1984). Over half of the therapists surveyed selected these two items as sources of stress. Although there was no item dealing specifically with client assaultive behavior, the expression of client anger toward the therapist also ranked high and was selected by over half of the subjects. It is certainly easy to understand how upsetting it can be if a client a therapist is treating expresses strong anger toward the therapist. It is my belief that assasultive behavior would be an even greater source of threat to therapists, but such potential clients may not seek out psychotherapy and also may not be accepted for therapy with any high frequency, particularly in an outpatient setting. However, because client expression of anger was mentioned, I discuss it further.

I hypothesize that there is more than one possible cause for a client expressing anger toward the therapist. For most clients, this would be a somewhat unusual occurrence, because the psychotherapist has a certain status as a socially sanctioned healer who is usually addressed as doctor, and also because clients want to be on good terms with their potential source of help. However, there are some clients whose difficulties center around hostile interactions with others. When dealing with such individuals, the therapist must expect open expressions of hostility, anger, and criticism. These are manifestations of the client's problems with others and clearly need to be handled by the therapist as part of the therapeutic process. As discussed in an earlier section, the therapist can point out to the client his or her actual problematic behavior in the therapeutic situation and how it is self-defeating. Essentially, the client's anger and related behaviors are to be expected and have influenced the goals of therapy. In this type of situation, at least theoretically, the client's anger should not be overly upsetting to the therapist, although no one likes to be a recipient of anger, and therapists, like clients, vary greatly in terms of their own personalities. Therapists who have difficulty in working with such clients probably should not accept them for therapy.

In those instances where the client's anger is unanticipated, the therapist is most likely to be upset. In situations of this type, it is not easy for the therapist to remain cool and detached, nor is it usually helpful to tell the client that his or her anger is displaced anger from an earlier period of life. As in all other comparable situations, the therapist must analyze the situation and try to determine what has produced or contributed to this display of anger. Has the particular subject discussed been a highly charged topic that somehow stimulated this degree of client response? Has the therapist unwittingly contributed to this expression of anger by a lack of sensitivity and misunderstanding of what the client was trying to communicate? Has the therapist misjudged the client's capacity for confrontation? Have the therapist's comments or interpretations been overly critical or been received in this fashion? These are some of the questions and self-scrutiny that the therapist might engage in when the client exhibits unusually strong anger toward him or her.

As noted, although client expressions of anger have been mentioned as one of the most stressful events for psychotherapists, I am not sure if they occur with a high frequency, at least in most outpatient psychotherapy settings. It is of course possible that clients may react differently to different therapists depending on age, sex, reputation, and personal style. In my own experience both as a therapist and as a supervisor, I recall only a few instances of such client behavior, and the director of our university psychological service center states that her experience is similar to mine. However, I do recall two such cases and relate one of them briefly, because it illustrates the effect of such client behavior on one therapist.

This particular case concerned a client with whom I had great difficulty. He would fluctuate somewhat between being aggressively hostile and being depressed. I, in turn, despite attempting to be the perfect therapist, fluctuated between being sympathetic and concerned when he was depressed and trying to control my own negative feelings when he would become critical of me. On one occasion, he surprised me by saying rather critically that he wanted me to take his case seriously. When I asked him why he thought I didn't take his case seriously, he told me that when he looked up at me I usually was smiling. Actually, when he looked up at me he exhibited what I interpreted as a smile and I tended to respond in a like manner. He interpreted this as my making light of his difficulties. I have to admit that I became angry at what I thought was very unfair criticism, and apparently my anger showed, for the client said, "Now I've made you angry." I denied this in an angry manner, saying, "The hell you have!" As soon as I said this, I knew I had acted poorly, and I then admitted my feelings and the reasons for them. I learned from this experience how anger and criticism expressed by a client can have a very upsetting influence on the therapist.

Strong emotions expressed by others clearly have an impact, and anger expressed by a client can lead to anger or fear on the part of the therapist. The therapist must recognize, acknowledge, and try to understand these emotions and how they affect the ongoing therapy. Sometimes, the therapist's being open about personal feelings and admitting his or her humanity may be therapeutic for the client. At other times, this may not be indicated, and the therapist should attempt as honestly and objectively as possible to evaluate the impact of the client's anger on both him or herself and the therapy. If such a problem becomes overly intrusive and seriously interferes with the therapist's ability to work effectively, some means of resolving the impasse needs to be secured. Unfortunately, in a case of this type the client's view that most people are difficult to deal with may be reinforced. However, if the client cannot participate effectively as a collaborator in the therapeutic undertaking and produces considerable stress in the therapist, there is little to be gained by continued meetings and continued emotional confrontations. A mutually satisfactory therapeutic relationship is essential for significant therapeutic gain. Fortunately, cases of the kind described here are not frequently encountered in outpatient brief psychotherapy.

Before concluding this section, I mention one other potential problem or crisis situation that conceivably could arise during the process of psychotherapy. This pertains to threats verbalized during therapy by the client against others. In the now famous case of *Tarasoff v. Regents of the University of California*, the Supreme Court of California ruled that when a therapist determines that a patient is a serious threat to others in terms of violence, "he or she has a duty to exercise reasonable care to protect the forseeable victim of the danger. While predicting violence is difficult, the court felt that the risk to potential victims outweighs the need of the client" (Pryzwansky & Wendt, 1987, p. 96).

In this particular case, a client was receiving therapy from a psychologist at a student mental health clinic. During therapy, the client several times threatened to use a gun against his former girlfriend. The therapist did recognize that the situation was serious. He informed the campus police, who took the client into custody. However, they felt the client was not really disturbed, and evaluations made by supervising psychiatrists also agreed that commitment was not necessary. Unfortunately, the client later proceeded to kill his former girlfriend.

In discussing this case, Pryzwansky and Wendt (1987) made the following points: "Practitioners need to be aware that the duty is to 'protect' the potential victim, which does not necessarily mean directly warning the person. The protection conceivably includes other reasonable methods, such as notifying the police, removing instruments/harm, continuous supervision by the family or community, modifying treatment, referral, or even commitment" (p. 96).

It is not surprising, therefore, that the Tarasoff decision has generated considerable discussion and concern among mental health practitioners. It intrudes on the traditional privacy and confidentiality of the therapeutic relationship. However, the courts evidently have taken the view that the possibility of serious harm being inflicted on others by a client in therapy overrides the issue of confidentiality and places a certain responsibility on the therapist. Therapists also need to make this responsibility clear to their clients.

CONTEMPLATING FUTURE TERMINATION

At some point after therapy is well under way, the possibility of termination at some future date must be given some consideration. This type of consideration comes into play much sooner and more naturally in brief forms of psychotherapy. If the therapist is working in a setting where specific time limits are followed, then the precise termination session is announced at the beginning of therapy and is clearly anticipated. In fact, a number of therapists, beginning with Otto Rank, have advocated the setting of time limits as facilitating the therapeutic process, and a number of clinical settings use a therapeutic approach with specified time limits. Whether or not a specific time limit is followed, such as 10, 20, or 30 sessions, most practitioners of brief psychotherapy have some range of therapy sessions in mind as the usual or expected length of psychotherapy—and if they don't, their clients will.

Because clients and their problems vary, it is to be expected that without specific time limits the duration of psychotherapy will also vary, even when the therapy is relatively brief. Consequently, the therapist must be alert to how therapy is proceeding and to any indications that the possibility of termination should be considered. I discuss the matter of termination in greater detail later, but the issue is raised here because it is during the interim or main phase of psychotherapy that the first possible consideration of termination may arise. The goal of therapy generally is to facilitate and encourage the independent functioning of the client and not to foster dependency on the therapist. Therefore, the therapist needs to be sensitive to issues of this type.

CONCLUDING SUMMARY

In this chapter, the focus has been on the interim, middle, or major phase of psychotherapy, that is, the phase between the very early sessions and the eventual termination of therapy. An attempt has been made to provide the reader with some understanding of the psychotherapeutic process and the kinds of problems that may be anticipated in the normal practice of psychotherapy. Occasional brief case excerpts from my own professional experience have been used to illustrate the topics discussed.

Although a teacher or practitioner may want to provide as specific and concrete a guide as possible for learning and conducting psychotherapy, this is not always possible. Although there are psychotherapeutic approaches that have been developed for specific disorders, and some of them appear to be highly structured—for example, Session 1, Session 2, and so forth, I question whether therapy actually proceeds in this type of fashion in most real-life situations.

As emphasized throughout this book, there is too much variation among clients and their life situations to be able to use exactly the same approach in precisely the same way for every client with somewhat similar problems. All therapy does not proceed in exactly the same way, even though there are certain variables that are common among the different forms of psychotherapy and that appear to have a therapeutic impact. Even where specific therapeutic techniques appear to be indicated in working with certain client problems, the exact process with different clients will not be exactly the same. The therapist, of course, needs to be knowledgeable about the psychotherapy process and outcome and be capable of formulating a workable plan for therapy and of selecting procedures that are most efficacious for the problem at hand. At the same time, he or she must evaluate the process of therapy, be sensitive to problems that come up in therapy, and be able to resolve such problems and modify his or her approach as necessary. Psychotherapy is an active process that requires all the attention and cogitation of which a therapist is capable.

Chapter 7

Terminating Therapy

Termination is a natural phase of the psychotherapeutic process. Just as all living things at some point must reach a natural termination, so must psychotherapy. Consequently, termination should be anticipated by the therapist as a regular ending sequence of psychotherapy, and at some point the client also will begin to entertain the idea of ending therapy. It is true that if therapy has gone well and a very positive relationship has developed between therapist and client, some emotional features of separation may be experienced. This, too, can be viewed as a normal phenomenon, if not overly strong, and accepted on a realistic basis for what it is—a parting of two individuals who have shared some important experiences together. How termination actually takes place, however, may vary from case to case, and in this chapter I examine the factors that may influence the termination process.

PLANNING FOR TERMINATION

Termination obviously will vary with different clients and with the accompanying variations in how the psychotherapy has been conducted. The termination process where therapy has progressed smoothly and positively may be expected to differ from that where therapy has been problematic and unsuccessful. In some instances, as I know from personal experience as well as from a review of the research literature (Garfield, 1986), the therapist has no particular problem in planning for termination—the client has made the decision apparently on his or her own and has terminated without informing the therapist or giving any advanced notice. As discussed previously, a significant percentage of outpatients will terminate prematurely by failing to show up for future appointments. I used to advise my students and interns to go over their notes and tapes of such cases and try to see if they could have missed possible indicators of such premature termination. Although it is possible to point to some likely causes retrospectively, I'm not sure how beneficial this process is in significantly reducing future dropouts from psychotherapy. In any event, on the basis of past experience, there will be clients who drop out of therapy after just a few interviews, and they will handle the problem of termination all by themselves.

In settings where brief, time-limited therapy is practiced, there should be a clearly anticipated and smoothly handled termination for most clients. The therapy is brief, and clients are informed at the outset that therapy will be terminated at the end of a designated session, for example, the 10th session. In such instances, there is a natural anticipated termination point, and it does have some advantages. Both participants in therapy know they have a specified and limited amount of time in which to try and secure some type of positive outcome. This has been seen by some as having a very positive motivational effect on the therapeutic process (Koss & Butcher, 1986). Regardless of its potential therapeutic effect, it does signify at the outset the time limits of therapy and when termination can be anticipated.

In much of psychotherapy, however, no specific termination date is mentioned, or some future possible time is referred to in a vague manner. In these instances, more consideration must be given to the matter of termination by the therapist. The therapist must consider, first of all, when to bring the matter up for discussion with the client. He or she must also plan how to discuss the matter and how to handle it. Because termination is an important part of the therapeutic process, it needs as much planning and skillful handling as other important aspects of psychotherapy.

In most cases, termination should not present any real problems. This would be particularly so if reference was made to an approximate termination date in the first session or in one of the other early sessions. Also, because the length of treatment in brief therapy is, by definition, brief, there is less opportunity for overly strong attachment to the therapist (or the client), although individual variations in this regard do exist. Nevertheless, the therapist should consider the implications for termination of each case and plan accordingly.

POSSIBLE PROBLEMS

There are at least three sets of variables and their possible interactions that need to be considered in terms of termination: client variables, therapist variables, and length of therapy. Although these are discussed separately, they can and do interact, and in such cases the effect on termination as well as on other aspects of psychotherapy is increased.

Client Variables

Clients can be expected to vary in terms of their dependence on therapy and the therapist. For most of them, other factors being equal, termination is an expected and nontraumatic event. This is particularly true if a positive outcome has been secured. On the other hand, for those clients who are extremely dependent, who have few outside support systems, and/or who have developed a strong attachment to the therapist, termination can be an anxiety-provoking event. This type of dependency may also be accentuated by the length of therapy and the particular role taken by the therapist. Therapy that lasts for a long time and is measured in years instead of weeks is more likely to increase the dependency of the client and his or her reliance on therapy as a regular part of life. In such situations, separation anxiety and feelings of being abandoned by the therapist may indeed emerge.

In brief psychotherapy, as already indicated, such a pattern is much less likely. Nevertheless, the therapist should be aware of this possibility with certain clients. He or she should avoid reinforcing overly dependent behavior on the part of the client. Also, with such dependent clients, the therapist clearly must pay more attention to preparing the client for therapy and for the eventual separation from the therapist. One procedure that can be used to limit such problems is to stagger the last few visits. Thus, if sessions have been held on a weekly basis, the frequency and intensity of therapy can be reduced by scheduling the last few appointments for every 2 weeks. The following brief case summaries illustrate this practice.

A.B. was a 40-year-old male who at first resisted any psychological explanation for his difficulties and tended to emphasize somatic complaints. I predicted that he would drop out of therapy early—but I was wrong. After a number of difficult sessions where he seemed to be somewhat resistive and negative toward therapy, but never against me personally, he began to change slowly. He was always prompt for his appointments, he never missed any, and he was very deferential to me. Because of the particular problems involved and the way therapy developed, I saw him for a moderately long time, about 80 weekly sessions. When he seemed to have made noticeable progress, I brought up the matter of termination. He reacted very strongly to this suggestion, saying that he did not believe he was really ready to leave therapy, and other statements of this type. As a result of this discussion, I told

him that we would continue, but on a staggered basis, and we would
see how he got along. He agreed to this, and the next appointment was
scheduled for 2 weeks later. When seen at that time, he related that
despite his misgivings, he had gotten along without real difficulty. As a
result of his report, the next session was set for 3 weeks hence, and after
a couple of additional staggered visits the case was terminated very
amicably.

The preceding case was presented even though the therapy does not
qualify as brief therapy. It illustrates, however, the potential problem of
overdependence on the therapist and its potential implications for the
process of termination. In this case, the staggered visits worked out
quite successfully and appeared to increase the patient's self-confidence
in his ability to handle his life situation on his own.

In another case, a young woman was seen on a weekly basis for 16
sessions. Because of travel and holiday arrangements, these sessions
occurred over a period of about 6 months. I had mentioned the
possibility of termination after the 16th session during the 13th and 15th
sessions, and there did not appear to be any problems about it. She
nodded in apparent acceptance of this. However, during the 16th
session, she said she would feel better if we could have one more
session. After a brief discussion, I agreed but suggested we schedule the
extra session for 4 weeks later. This would give us time to see how well
she would be getting along. She finally agreed to this plan, and the
appointment was duly noted. About 5 days before the scheduled visit,
she called to say she was getting along well and saw no need for the
extra visit—and that concluded matters.

The therapist thus must be keenly aware of the type of client with
whom he or she is dealing and the needs of the client that are being
served by the therapy. Where the therapist suspects that the client is
unduly dependent and reliant on the therapist, it seems desirable to
bring up the matter of future termination relatively early in therapy and
to deal with it in an appropriate and realistic manner. With most other
clients, as noted, there will be little difficulty. Many clients will be
anticipating termination, and some will even suggest it, directly or
indirectly, before it is even broached by the therapist.

It is also likely that termination may be more of a problem with
children, particularly where a very strong attachment to the therapist
has taken place. Children are more dependent, and when warmth and
affection have been limited, they may be more likely to become
emotionally attached to the therapist as an important source of gratification. Although I have not worked with children for many years, I have
supervised graduate students who have worked in children's settings
and have had occasion to observe such attachments. In such instances,

it is important that undue dependency not be fostered and eventual termination be referred to as an expected, natural, and realistic part of the therapy experience.

Therapist Variables

The second category of variables that may influence the process of termination pertains to the therapist and his or her role in therapy. Sometimes, the therapist may contribute, consciously or unconsciously, to possible difficulties with respect to termination. Some individual therapists, because of their own personal needs, may receive gratification from the patient's dependency and actually foster or reinforce such behavior. Such a therapeutic relationship makes a normal ending of therapy more difficult and creates other problems as well.

In other instances, the therapist may become overly involved with the patient—what the psychoanalysts have referred to as a problematic countertransference. In this situation, the therapist finds the relationship with the patient very satisfying and is reluctant to give it up. The patient may or may not be a truly willing participant in this relationship. However, termination of therapy becomes more difficult when the patient brings up the subject or when a previously set date for termination comes up. This clearly is not a desirable state of affairs. It impairs the therapist's objectivity, ability to listen, to respond empathically, and above all to conduct therapy in terms of the best interests of the patient. When the therapist, for whatever reason, wants to continue the relationship beyond what is therapeutically desirable, his or her sensitivity to the communications of the patient is diminished. The patient may communicate readiness for termination in several ways, but the therapist somehow does not "hear" these communications.

As an example, I refer to a case that I was supervising. The client was a woman in her mid-twenties who was being seen by a male graduate student. She had sought psychotherapeutic help because of feelings of depression and difficulties with her boyfriend. She was a bright, motivated, and reasonably integrated young woman who responded well to psychotherapy and made good progress. Around the ninth interview, she stated that she was getting along quite well. This important communication seemingly was not attended to or was overlooked by the therapist. Later in the same interview, the client asked how much longer therapy would continue. She did not really get a clear response to this query from the therapist.

During the following supervisory session, I pointed out these two interactions to the therapist. I emphasized that the client's statements centered around the possible termination of therapy and that he, the therapist, appeared to disregard completely and fail to respond to these important communications. I also suggested that the client had been a favorable one to work with, and I could understand how the therapist might be reluctant to terminate her therapy. At the same time, I indicated that by not listening to the client and not responding to these communications, the therapist was not fulfilling his professional responsibilities. When he said that he understood what I was saying, I told him that if the client did not bring up any references to termination during the next session, he should do so when there was 15 to 20 minutes left, so the matter could be discussed.

I was pleased and reassured as a result of this supervisory session and was interested to see what would take place during the next session. The client was not too active, did not really refer to termination in any way, and to my surprise, neither did the therapist. He had a somewhat difficult time explaining things to me during the next supervisory session, and instead of being my natural critical self, I restrained myself. I told him in a good-natured way that if termination was not discussed in the very next session, he should consider transferring to some other doctoral clinical program.

This story does have a happy ending. In the next session, the client again brought up the matter of ending therapy, because she felt she was not having any serious problems and believed she had secured what she wanted from therapy. My student had learned his lesson by this time and made me proud by agreeing with the client and terminating her therapy with this session. I should add that this student therapist was very bright, related well to his clients, and had promise as an effective therapist. In this situation, however, because therapy was quite successful, relatively brief, and because he secured considerable satisfaction from his role as a successful therapist, he found it difficult to listen to communications that signalled a possible end to therapy. This is a potential problem to which both experienced and novice therapists must be sensitive to and alertly aware.

A somewhat related problem may also be discernible at times. I refer to situations where a therapist believes that a client isn't quite ready to terminate therapy, that more gains can be secured from additional psychotherapy, or that if the client should stop seeing the therapist, the consequences would be dreadful. Again, it seems clear that the personal needs of individual psychotherapists may strongly influence their appraisal and conduct of therapy. Because of this, therapists must strive to listen to clients and to think about them in as objective a fashion as possible. A study conducted at the Minneapolis Veterans Administration Mental Hygiene Clinic of patients kept in therapy for a long time illustrates this problem (Stieper & Weiner, 1959, 1965). In studying some

300 patients, it was reported that the great majority of so-called interminable patients were actually being seen by a small number of the clinic therapists. These therapists were characterized as follows:

> . . . therapist primarily desires to "help," and this feeling can be sustained indefinitely; tends to personalize relationship; tends to aim for marked changes in very sick patients; desires to succeed with intensive therapy; and needs to feel appreciated and effective (as a person and as a therapist). None of the comments made by the judges suggested that the therapists were dealing with chronic patients who required interminable support. (Stieper & Wiener, 1965, p. 66)

In this situation, the clinic administrators made a decision to terminate a number of the cases that had been in therapy for a long time. The therapists of these patients responded that they had kept the patients out of the hospital all this time and that terminating the therapy of these patients would result in their hospitalization. Nevertheless, the patients were in fact discharged. A follow-up study indicated that the hospitalization and relapse rates for these patients did not differ from those of any comparable group of patients (Stieper & Wiener, 1959, 1965). In actuality, most of them were able to get along without psychotherapy and without requiring hospitalization.

The results of this study illustrate quite clearly how the needs of some therapists may influence how they view their clients and thus maintain their treatment. With students in training, as I have indicated, it is not uncommon that some of them become overly attached to their clients, and for these student-therapists termination appears to be a painful process. Some have even offered to stay on beyond the required practicum time in order to prolong the therapy. Even though attempts are made to show the student what is occurring in such cases, the attempts may not be fully successful.

Thus, apart from client dependency issues, there are also potential problems in terms of the therapist's views and response to possible termination, even in brief therapy. If the client should bring up possible termination relatively early in therapy because he or she feels progress has been made and results have been secured, the therapist may state that not enough has been done. The client's response may even be viewed as a form of resistance. If the client should exhibit very quick improvement, psychodynamically oriented therapists might be inclined to view this as a "flight into health," another form of resistance. A somewhat similar view may be taken if the client wants to terminate because of lack of progress. In this instance, the therapist may view such behavior as resistance, because not enough time has been devoted to the therapy and the client has not been sufficiently involved in the therapy.

Some therapists are inclined to avoid terminating therapy after a reasonable period of therapy (20 therapy sessions or so) when there has been no demonstrable improvement, even though termination might be in the best interests of the client. A variety of motives may be involved, and it is very important that the psychotherapist strive to be as objective as possible and truly place the welfare of the client first. Sometimes, a therapist may have feelings of guilt at abandoning a client at such a point, even though he or she may feel somewhat inadequate in the handling of the case. In some instances, the matter of a steady income, although not consciously verbalized, may also influence the therapist in terms of possible termination. Terminating a client when no meaningful progress has been secured also signifies failure to the therapist, and although all therapists should realistically not anticipate success with every case, it may be difficult for many to acknowledge failure. Nevertheless, it is my view that if a reasonable period of time has elapsed with little or no progress, for example, 20 to 25 interviews, the situation should be discussed with the client and termination suggested. How this might be done is discussed later.

Length of Therapy

The third set of variable that may influence or contribute to possible problems of termination pertains to the length and intensity of treatment. Clearly, in long-term psychotherapy, particularly when it occurs several times a week, there is a greater potential for a more intensive relationship as well as a therapy-fostered dependency on the part of the patients. Consequently, termination is more of a problem in such instances, and issues such as separation anxiety and the like are more likely to be encountered. The length and intensity of therapy will also interact with client and therapist variables. The worst scenario would appear to involve a dependent patient and a need-fulfilling possessive therapist engaged in long-term intensive psychotherapy. Problems of this type are considerably less possible in briefer forms of psychotherapy, but therapists need to be sensitive to their possible occurrence.

CONSIDERATIONS IN PLANNING
FOR TERMINATION

Generally, it is a good procedure to give the client at the start of therapy some estimate of how long therapy can be expected to last. If the problems presented by the client are not particularly troublesome and the overall prognosis appears to be good, the therapist can mention the briefer end of the brief therapy range, for example, 12 to 20 sessions, as a probable estimate. If the probabilities are not as favorable, a somewhat longer estimate can be given, perhaps 25 sessions or so. In this way, the situation is not amorphous, and the client has some idea of what is involved both in terms of time and money. The therapist can also add that a better estimate probably can be made after 3 or 4 sessions. Such statements not only give the client a realistic estimate of how long therapy may last, but also convey the idea of some termination point— therapy will not be forever.

During therapy, the client may ask questions or make comments that have a direct or indirect bearing on matters pertaining to termination. Such items should be discussed and attempts made to ascertain what has motivated the comment or query. For example, if the client should remark that therapy is too long or that the progress is very slow, the therapist should try to clarify the client's feelings about therapy that may engender such comments. Is the client voicing dissatisfaction with therapy, is he or she communicating a desire to terminate, or does the comment about slow progress mask a fear about ending therapy with little change?

As noted, any reference by the client to therapy or the therapist should be explored without delay to try to understand the basis for the client's statements. Obviously, some communications are clearer and easier to understand than others, but the therapist should try to be fairly confident that he or she does understand what the client is communicating or trying to communicate. The question, "When do we quit?" could be related to the client's feeling sufficiently improved. As such, it readily translates to, "Aren't we approaching the end of therapy?" On the other hand, it might also signify some dissatisfaction with therapy. The message here could be that the time is going by or getting close to the end, and "When do I get better?" Consequently, the therapist must be sensitive to all possible meanings and attempt to clarify the client's communications in order to fully understand what is being communicated.

If no particular problems are apparent as therapy proceeds, a reference to future termination can be made when it would be natural to mention it in therapy; for example, in relation to a forthcoming event or to a related matter being discussed. If termination has been linked with a future move, graduation, new job, or some other event, it can be mentioned in passing when such events are discussed. Termination is then more likely to be viewed as a normally occurring event and to be anticipated in that light. If there are no such opportunities, the therapist should mention the future termination date about three to five sessions before the last session, depending on the length of therapy. It can be mentioned again at the end of the next-to-last session. Such comments should be made in a brief and matter of fact way as a reminder of the time remaining.

In the case of an overly dependent client or a client that the therapist expects might experience termination as an upsetting experience, it is probably advisable to bring up the matter of termination earlier in therapy. In such a case, the therapist can also discuss the client's dependency as a general problem that the client has by illustrating his or her dependent behavior in therapy and with specific reference to his or her probable response to termination. One goal of therapy would be to lessen the client's dependency, and how termination is handled would be an important part of therapy as well as a partial criterion of outcome.

With some clients, the termination process is facilitated by tapering the last few sessions. Where weekly sessions have been used, the therapist can schedule the last couple of sessions at 2-week intervals or 3-week intervals, as appropriate. This extends the termination process and helps to make it a more gradual process. If therapy has been quite brief, consisting of 8 to 12 sessions, it may not be necessary to taper the last couple of sessions. Again, how the therapist handles this matter will depend on his or her evaluation of the client. I once treated a veteran whose primary referral problem was severe stammering. He was slightly below average in intelligence, worked as a laborer in a large industrial plant, was married, and had acquired a physical disability during his military service. In part because of his speech problem, he had few social acquaintances or contacts. Although by most criteria he was not considered a prime candidate for psychotherapy, he was cooperative despite being somewhat passive and was a very likeable person. Actually, I admired the way this person handled his difficulties and maintained a rather positive outlook on life despite his deficits. He seemed to be positive about attending the therapy sessions, even though we made only modest progress at best. After about 30 sessions, I decided that little more would be gained by continuing therapy, and that we should consider termination. We had reached a plateau, and I was afraid that the patient was becoming somewhat dependent on me. Consequently, I pointed out that we probably would secure little additional gain by continuing therapy, and that we should plan on ending therapy. The patient agreed with my analysis but also requested that I see him at least occasionally before we terminated. Because I was being promoted and transferred to another city in 5 months, I agreed to see him a few additional times on a monthly basis instead of a weekly one and for 30 minutes instead of our usual 50-minute hour. He agreed to this, and I saw him for four additional abbreviated monthly sessions. He was positive about this arrangement, and we parted on very amicable terms. The amount of extra time provided was small and seemed to lead to a positive ending.

Although I believe that therapy should not be continued beyond a point of no return therapeutically, I also feel strongly that termination needs to be handled sensitively but in a clear and definite manner. In doing so, however, the therapist needs to respond to the particular patient and how termination may be viewed or used by the patient. If the patient, in response to a mention of future termination, complains of being abandoned and cast aside, the therapist should try to clarify the patient's unrealistic expectations or desires.

Although dependent or demanding patients are frequently the source of such problems, the therapist should also examine his or her behavior for any possible influence in this regard. In cases being seen by students in one children's clinic over a period of time, it was reasonably clear that the clinic staff's expectation was that all children would find the students' departure at the end of the semester to be a traumatic event. As a result, the student therapists were instructed by their local supervisors to prepare the children for this calamitous event by telling the children far in advance of termination and repeating frequently that they were going to be very unhappy when therapy ended. At least some of these therapists did a good job of convincing the children that they would be unhappy, and many of the children did respond as expected. Although I agree that therapists should prepare patients for termination, they should not overdo this by convincing them that they will be at least partially devastated by having to terminate therapy. In the illustration provided, the children seemingly learned what the expected response was, and in many cases did respond in the expected direction, in line with the repeated warnings or instructions.

Most clients will be influenced by what they are told by the therapist and by any cues they receive. Consequently, if the therapist deals with termination in a matter of fact manner, it is likely that the client will model the therapist's behavior and that therapy will be concluded without too many histrionics or difficulties. Termination is best viewed as a desired and naturally occurring anticipated event.

I see no great need to recapitulate in the last session what has been discussed in therapy or to give the client an intellectual summary of his or her past problems and limitations. However, it is worthwhile to review briefly the problems that brought the client to therapy, what progress had been made in overcoming these problems, and things that the client should try to continue working on under his or her own initiative. Ending therapy doesn't necessarily mean that the client can't continue to make some progress on his or her own. In fact, helping the client to be able to cope independently and effectively with future adjustment difficulties should be a desired goal of most therapy. Thus, cognitions and behaviors that have contributed to the client's difficulties should be curtailed and other more effective patterns used to cope with the problems that arise. If the client learns something in therapy that can be applied constructively to his or her current and future life situation, then that therapy can be judged as truly effective.

LACK OF PROGRESS AND TERMINATION

As indicated earlier, despite a lack of progress, the responsible therapist must consider termination when the chances for securing change appear minimal. Although every therapist wants to help every client, at some point he or she also must face reality. Clearly, deciding on termination in such a situation is not easy, but it needs to be considered seriously. To prolong therapy when either it is no longer required or it appears to have little likelihood of helping the patient is clearly not in the best interests of the patient.

Consequently, after a reasonable attempt at psychotherapy has been made and little positive change has been secured, the issue of termination should be squarely faced and discussed with the client. At such a time, several different possibilities or recommendations can be considered. One possibility is to consider additional therapy with a different therapist at the present time or at some time in the future. In choosing this option, the therapist should have some basis for believing that such a referral would have a reasonable probability of securing a positive outcome. It is important that the therapist be honest and accurate in his or her appraisals and recommendations in such a situation. If the therapist feels that the client is going to be little helped by psychotherapy, then it does not seem ethical or feasible to suggest further psychotherapy. To do so would simply be passing responsibility to someone else. It also would be unrealistic and unfair to the client. Furthermore, if the client does not bring up the issue of seeking additional help, the therapist should be very careful about introducing this matter. Most clients have concerns about themselves and are without high degrees of self-esteem. Thus, the therapist should not want to increase the client's self-concerns by recommending additional therapy unless he or she sincerely believes it will be helpful to the client.

If, however, the client does appear to need further help, the therapist should discuss this and evaluate the client's thoughts and feelings about termination and the apparent need for additional help. In this instance, the therapist must evaluate the client's total situation and try to offer some suggestions that may be helpful. For example, if the therapist is not very interested in or adept at introducing some specific behavioral techniques that could be potentially useful, this could be discussed frankly with the client. Depending on the client's response, a referral could be made to a different therapist. If the client seems opposed to any suggestions for additional treatment, it is wise not to argue with the client or try to force him or her to seek such additional therapy. The therapist must be sensitive to the client's views and perceptions. Arguing with a client, particularly at the final therapy session, is not a good procedure.

An approach that may be useful where not very much positive change has occurred is to face the facts squarely but sympathetically. The client can be told to see how things work out for a few months. If, after that time, the client would like an additional trial of therapy, he or she can call the therapist or the clinic and can be referred to seek therapy elsewhere if he or she prefers. If other treatments seem indicated, they should be mentioned and possible referral help given. If the client is quite disturbed or distressed, then clearly a proper referral should be made.

CONCLUDING COMMENTS

In this chapter we have considered the matter of terminating therapy, some of the considerations that enter into such a decision, various means of instituting the formal ending of psychotherapy, and some of the problems that may arise. The following points in particular were emphasized:

1. The therapist should make some reference to termination well before the last therapy session and be sure that the client is fully aware of what is to occur.
2. The therapist needs to consider the particular client, the length of therapy, and the type of relationship developed.
3. The therapist must be cognizant of his or her role in the relationship and handle matters accordingly. The welfare of the client always must be given the main priority.
4. In considering termination, the therapist should evaluate whatever decisions and referrals seem most appropriate.
5. In most cases, termination can be handled smoothly and without any particular stresses or strains. It should be looked forward to as a natural and desirable goal.

Chapter 8
Some Post-Therapy Considerations

After therapy has been concluded, it is useful to prepare a brief summary of the case. This has many potentially positive values. It allows the therapist to review what has occurred during the therapy sessions and to make some appraisal of both the treatment and the outcome. It also provides a summary of the therapy, which serves a recordkeeping function as well as a potential report of the therapy to other interested parties. Even though preparing such a summary requires some additional time, the project is worth the extra time invested in it.

Although the therapist has a fairly good idea of how well the client has performed in the therapy, it is a sound procedure to sit back and try to evaluate the outcome of the therapy as objectively as possible. It would be even more desirable and more objective to use a variety of validated measures to assess outcome at the termination of therapy, but this is not a practical procedure in most clinical situations. Selecting appropriate measures is also a complex task. Therefore, the therapist must use the procedures or sources of information that are most readily available. The sources available are the comments of the client, case notes, observations of the client, and any other inputs the therapist may have received from significant others. If a regular brief self-rating scale is used such as the Beck Depression Inventory (Beck, Ward, Mendelson, Mock, & Erbaugh, 1961), this also would form a source of input for the therapist's evaluation.

Before discussing the matter of post-therapy appraisal further, I mention a few points about therapy notes. Most references to therapy notes and records that I have seen have discussed them mainly in relation to possible malpractice suits and court proceedings. However, my frame of reference here is in terms of evaluating therapeutic work and particularly in trying to improve it. Thus, I try to note down as soon as possible after the session two types of information. One lists what appeared to be the important or outstanding events or interactions that occurred during the hour. These can center around the specific content, cognitions, affects, or behaviors that highlighted the session. They can refer to the client, to me, or to both. The other type of item that I try to note down concerns my appraisal of what went on, what problems seem to be evident or imminent, where I think therapy is heading, what I should be particularly sensitive to during future sessions, and the like.

The aforementioned notations need not take a lot of time or a great deal of space. The various items can be listed or referred to briefly. Perfect grammar and the "King's English" are not required. What are required are careful observations, accurate recall, and adequate thought.

Brief, cryptic, and meaningful notations not only allow the therapist to keep current with the ongoing therapy but also to monitor it as well. Particularly, when a specific problem arises in therapy that was not anticipated, it is sometimes helpful and instructive to check back over these notes to see if the problem might have been anticipated. Whether or not this occurs, the notes available at the end of therapy provide some basis for trying to evaluate one's therapy. Although the more formal and systematic attempts at evaluating outcome have not been without their problems and critics, attempts at evaluation are important (Bergin, 1971; Eysenck, 1966; Garfield, 1983a; Smith et al., 1980). Systematic research, however, is obviously complex and is far removed from the attempts at evaluation suggested here for the individual therapist. Nevertheless, some type of evaluation is necessary if the therapist is to secure some appraisal or feedback concerning his or her therapeutic efforts. It is also important if the therapist is to profit from experience and improve the quality of his or her psychotherapeutic work.

In order to make the process of evaluation more meaningful, some simple aids or guides can be devised for use. Simply to use overly crude or general types of categories for evaluation, however, is not very helpful. Such final evaluative judgments of therapy as "Improved" or "Some Improvement" are not informative. Both quantitatively and qualitatively, they are lacking in meaning. What the therapist ideally would like to know is: "Improved in what way and to what extent?"

In order to make graduate students in clinical psychology sensitive to the need for evaluating their own therapy cases, I devised a very simple form that they could complete and which requires relatively little time and effort. A copy is reproduced in Figure 8-1. Although the rating scale

Figure 8-1
Case Evaluation Form

Case _____ Sex _____ Age _____ Referred by _____

Therapist _____ Supervisor _____

No. of Interviews Seen _____ No. of Missed Appointments _____

Referral or treatment
problem(s) _____

_____

Possible changes at termination _____

_____

Recommendations for this case (if any) _____

_____

Rating Scales

1. *Amount of change in client*

   Please rate the *amount of change* you believe has occurred in this client since he/she started therapy. Please do *not* rate on this scale the final level of adjustment of the client. Rather, please rate the amount of *change* or difference in functioning you believe has occurred in this client since the beginning of therapy, regardless of how well or badly adjusted you believe the client currently is and how much or how little work might remain to be done in order for the client to be considered completely healthy and well functioning.

   _____ 1. Client has changed markedly for the worse.

   _____ 2. Client has changed somewhat for the worse.

   _____ 3. Client has changed slightly for the worse.

   _____ 4. Client has shown essentially no change.

   _____ 5. Client has changed slightly for the better.

   _____ 6. Client has changed somewhat for the better.

   _____ 7. Client has changed markedly for the better.

used is clearly influenced by the therapist's subjective judgment about the individual case, the first section of the evaluation form does focus attention on the presenting or referral problem and the possible changes that have occurred at termination. This represents an attempt to focus on specific indices of change and not on global appraisals of improvement that are influenced by the client's overall level of adjustment. Final global ratings of improvement without specific reference points tend generally to be more positive than difference scores derived from pre- and post-therapy ratings or tests (Garfield, Prager, & Bergin, 1971).

On the whole, the use of this form with practicum students seemed to work out satisfactorily. It helped to emphasize the need to evaluate therapeutic work with clients and to focus on the possible changes that may have occurred. A few unpublished projects conducted by students did contain analyses of the ratings secured for a sample of clients, and they seemed quite realistic to me. Most ratings varied around the values indicating some positive changes with very few clients rated as changing for the worse and less than 10% rated as markedly improved. Thus, it is possible for therapists to make somewhat objective appraisals of their relative success with the clients with whom they have worked in psychotherapy. This also is dependent on keeping as accurate and objective records or summaries of the individual therapy sessions as possible.

HOW WELL DID THE CLIENT REALLY DO?

As noted, an attempt to evaluate both the process and outcome of the psychotherapy by the psychotherapist is strongly recommended as a desirable practice. Because psychotherapy is an interpersonal process of some intensity, the psychotherapist cannot avoid a significant degree of personal involvement in the process. This in some ways almost forces the therapist to try to evaluate what is going on during therapy. However, this process largely occurs during the therapy hour when the therapist is fully engaged in interaction with the client. An appraisal after each session and at the termination of the case is recommended. The appraisal after each session should serve as a guide for the following sessions and should be modified as new observations and information require. The appraisal after therapy has ended differs from these appraisals in certain ways.

First, there is less urgency about an evaluation of a case that has been terminated. For better or for worse, the therapy has been concluded and the focus should be on what the therapist can learn from this particular case. Secondly, the therapist can try to be somewhat detached and strive for some degree of objectivity in the evaluation process. The use of some type of rating scale, as indicated earlier, is one means of facilitating this task. This is primarily useful, however, when the emphasis is on listing the specific changes that can be noted at the end of therapy. If the therapist has clearly stated his or her goals at the beginning of therapy in specific rather than global terms, the task of evaluating client change obviously becomes oriented to these goals. The process becomes a more natural and meaningful one. Furthermore, therapists should think of client change and improvement in terms of the specific changes sought at the start of psychotherapy and considered as the goals by both therapist and client. This matter deserves further discussion.

In the past, largely under the influence of psychodynamic theories of personality, goals tended to be stated in overly general terms stressing dynamic concepts and formulations. Thus, such goals as "character change," "the reconstruction of personality" and "where there is id there shall ego be" were considered as desirable. In contrast, symptomatic change was looked on as being superficial and temporary. If the true cause, an unconscious conflict, were not brought to light, substitute symptoms were assumed to make their appearance later. However, largely as a result of research reported by behavior therapists, such dire consequences have not been noted, and helping to remove a client's symptoms has come to be looked on quite favorably. Although a noted practitioner of brief dynamic psychotherapy such as David Malan (1976) claimed to secure dynamic changes as well as mere symptomatic change, a study by Mintz (1981) indicated a high correlation between the two supposedly different types of change.

Both the goals of therapy and the attempted evaluation of therapeutic change should be relatively specific and as operational as possible. If the client seeks therapy primarily because of being depressed, then a lessening of the depression becomes a goal of therapy, and improvement should be judged in terms of the extent of change in the desired direction. Vague, global, or overly general categorizations of change tell the therapist very little of value and in reality are essentially deceptive. There is little to be gained by the therapist in practicing self-deception. If little change has been secured, it is in the best interests of the client that the therapist see the situation for what it is and assume the necessary professional responsibility for deciding on the appropriate course of action. This is also best for the therapist in terms of securing as valid feedback as possible and for deriving the optimum learning obtainable from the specific therapeutic experience.

For the purpose of illustrating further this discussion of clinical appraisals of psychotherapy, I refer to a study of outpatient therapy reported some years ago (Garfield & Kurz, 1952). The clinical files of 560 patients who had received treatment were examined in order to analyze the evaluations provided by the therapists at the termination of therapy. Surprisingly, evaluations by the therapist were lacking in three quarters of the cases:

> In the 103 cases terminated and evaluated by the therapist, over 25 different evaluative terms were used. The latter included such descriptive categories as: "Improved, greatly improved, slightly improved, much improved, some improvement, maximum improvement, fair adjustment, symptomatic improvement, further treatment not required, seems to have adjusted, recovered, treatment completed successfully, etc." (Garfield & Kurz, 1952, p. 7)

The preceding quotation demonstrates the very limited utility of evaluative designations or terms that lack precise meaning or definition. It's hard to know exactly what "treatment completed successfully" actually means in terms of positive client change. A better understanding of what was accomplished would have been secured if the specific changes in the client's behavior, affect, or cognitions relative to the presenting problems were noted. In most cases, some positive change in specific areas may be noted, although the amount of change will not be uniform for all problems. However, evaluating the different specific changes not only provides the therapist with the most meaningful information about what has been accomplished, presumably as a result of therapy, but it also informs him or her about what changes seem the most difficult to secure. For example, a remark not infrequently made concerning attempts at psychodynamic therapy is that the patient secured insight into his or her problems, but the symptoms remained. In other words, the therapist might be able to get the patient to verbalize a different set of beliefs or perceptions but be unable to change his or her behavior. Analysts have long recognized that so-called intellectual insight is not adequate unless accompanied by other changes.

In this discussion I have consistently emphasized attending to the presenting complaint when attempting to evaluate therapeutic work. This is because it is easy for therapists to focus on other matters when there has been little change with reference to the presenting complaint. Thus, if a patient seeks therapy because of a fear of flying, the main criterion of outcome should be, can the patient now fly without fear? To say that there is some improvement at the end of therapy although the patient still will not fly or enter an airplane is really stretching matters to the point of self-deception. I have read case summaries where the therapist states that the patient has not overcome his anxieties but appears to get along better with his wife. Although it is understandable that people will try to view their efforts in the most favorable light, therapists should not be misled by such attempts. If a person seeks help because of a particular problem and the therapist acknowledges this as a valid reason for seeking therapy, then any evaluation of the therapy should focus mainly on how well or how much this presenting problem has improved. It is true that some problems are only acknowledged or become evident after psychotherapy is under way. These problems can be considered as equal to the presenting problems or even as replacements for the latter. However, the basis for appraisal still centers around the problems of the patient, and other considerations are secondary.

Thus far we have focused on therapist appraisals and factors that therapists need to consider in their evaluations of psychotherapy outcome. However, the client can also provide appraisals or judgments of outcome. Certainly, the therapist, during the therapeutic engagement, both seeks and receives information from the client concerning the client's progress. As all therapists know, clients vary in their expressiveness and attitudes toward authoritarian figures, and clear appraisals of the therapy may be muted in some instances and blared forth in others. Consequently, additional information can be secured by having the client fill out a brief rating scale or inventory. I have not used them in my own limited practice, but have devised and used several in research projects that I conducted in the past. As mentioned earlier, the Beck Depression Inventory is one such brief scale that does not deal with therapy per se but asks the client to rate his or her depression. If depression is a major complaint, such a scale can be one source of information about the severity of the depression. It is administered by Beck and his followers throughout the course of brief cognitive-behavior therapy, and changes can be noted over time. The therapist can also compare initial and final scores to evaluate the extent of change.

Using pre- and post-difference scores on inventories or rating scales provide one type of evaluative measure and can be of some value in appraising client change. Although used somewhat differently, a brief therapy rating scale can also provide information at the end of therapy. Pre-post measures usually deal with the client's symptoms or distress, whereas a therapy rating scale usually asks the client to make ratings about improvement or overall adjustment. These generally resemble the therapist rating scale illustrated earlier, and one example is provided in Figure 8-2. In completing this type of scale, the client evaluates how much he or she has been helped and indicates the changes secured.

Although both the therapist and the client have participated in the identical series of psychotherapy sessions, this by no means indicates that they have viewed the process in the same way or will make similar ratings. Several published studies indicate that the actual correlation

Figure 8–2
THERAPY RATING OF CHANGE – CLIENT FORM

Client's Name _____

How much change in you as a person has occurred since you started therapy or counseling? Check the item that best fits your case.

1. Changed for the worse _____

2. Essentially no change _____

3. Changed very little _____

4. Changed somewhat _____

5. Changed considerably _____

6. Changed markedly _____

Can you briefly describe what changes took place?

Date _____

between the two sets of ratings are frequently quite low. For example, in the study by Sloane et al. (1975), therapists' ratings correlated only .21 with the ratings made by the patients. Horenstein, Houston, and Holmes (1973) reported a nonsignificant correlation of .10 between the ratings of therapists and clients. On the other hand, Garfield, Prager, and Bergin (1971) secured a correlation of .44 between the two comparable sets of ratings. Still, these ratings indicate a relatively limited level of agreement in how treatment outcome is viewed by therapists and clients.

These findings at first were both surprising and somewhat disconcerting to me, because I would have expected a greater degree of agreement. However, it does seem evident that the two sets of participants in psychotherapy have different needs and also have different views of what occurs. It is for such reasons that a truly adequate appraisal of psychotherapy outcome requires a variety of measures that also reflect the viewpoints involved. Strupp and Hadley (1977) advocated what they termed a *tripartite model* of evaluating therapeutic outcomes. In this formulation, the social behavior of the individual is a concern of society, the personal feelings and views of the client constitute another dimension, and professional evaluations by mental health experts represent the third aspect or dimension. According to this view, all three viewpoints, society, the client, and the profession, are required for a truly adequate appraisal of outcome.

In most clinical situations, as I have mentioned, truly comprehensive appraisals will not be feasible. However, in addition to a therapist rating scale, therapists and clinical settings may want to make use of a brief scale completed by the client. In this way, more than one viewpoint of the outcome of therapy can be secured, recognizing of course that the methods used are crude ones. There is also a potential problem if the therapist or the therapist's personal secretary asks the client to complete the form. In this type of situation, at least a number of clients may be reluctant to express any strong negative feelings toward the therapy for fear of alienating the therapist or for appearing to be ungrateful. In a clinic setting where the rating form is handled by the clinic secretary, there is probably a greater likelihood of securing more truthful appraisals.

Another procedure that can be used in terms of learning more about how the client has viewed therapy is to have a form with a few open-ended questions pertaining to the therapy. Questions can be asked that are of particular interest to the therapist in terms of securing feedback on therapy. Examples of this kind are the following:

1. What aspects of therapy did you feel were most important in helping you?
2. What features did you feel were not particularly helpful?

3. Did you feel that the type of therapy was suited to your type of problem and why?
4. Other comments you would like to make.

Obviously, the type of questions or items that can be used will depend on the interests of the individual therapist. A brief client evaluation form can be devised without great difficulty for use in appraising change in psychotherapy. Such a form can combine a brief rating scale of outcome plus a few questions that attempt to secure information about the process of change. The brevity of the form is a factor in its favor, because clients are more likely to complete such forms than more lengthy and complicated ones.

WHAT THE THERAPIST CAN
LEARN FROM EACH CASE

The preceding section discussed some relatively simple techniques that can be used by the therapist in an attempt to evaluate his or her therapeutic efforts. Although the techniques described are far from scientific models of reliability and validity, they can be useful in helping the therapist secure some information about the adequacy of his or her professional functioning. This by itself is a worthwhile objective. However, if the therapist is motivated to want to learn more about his or her therapeutic performance, it is possible to focus on this objective as well. In other words, what can the therapist learn from the clients with whom he or she works?

The combination of the kind of after-therapy notations described earlier plus the use of brief rating scales can be a source of information from which the therapist can attempt to formulate hypotheses and deductions concerning his or her therapeutic effectiveness and the potential factors involved. There are several aspects of this procedure that can be potentially useful for self-appraisal and self-learning, and I describe them briefly.

One of the aspects of psychotherapy that surprised me early in my professional career was the awareness of a distinctly noticeable difference between some of my perceptions and those of some patients. Although this occurred in a relatively small number of patients, it had a strong impact upon me. It indicated that I was not as empathically attuned to these patients as I thought. In going over my notes and reflecting about these incidents, I learned something about why these incidents occurred. In one case, two factors became quite clear. The patient was less well integrated than I had thought, and thus I had made assumptions about his degree of understanding that were inaccurate. In addition, I could see that providing intellectual formulations and interpretations to this patient were very satisfying to me personally, but weren't that meaningful or therapeutic for the patient. As I have already indicated, I also have noticed this pattern manifested in the therapeutic work of some students and have tried to get them to recognize this aspect of their interactions in therapy.

The object of such appraisals clearly is to check on one's own therapeutic behavior and to increase self-knowledge. This is a useful procedure as long as the therapist doesn't overdo it. For example, in the illustration given previously, it became obvious to me that I particularly enjoyed giving explanations to certain patients. As someone who has done some teaching for most of his career, I could see that I was not averse to lecturing to patients as well as to students. Thus, I sensitized myself to this pattern of lecturing to patients. I also noted that I indulged in this practice mainly with some patients and not with others, and that with a few of the former group, therapy could get very intellectual while other aspects were somewhat neglected. This process of self-analysis, therefore, sharpened my therapeutic acumen and influenced my therapeutic behavior for the better, at least in my view.

If the therapist is frank and honest in noting down his or her reactions to the client and to the just-completed therapy hour, some increased understanding about how he or she responds to certain clients can be secured. For example, if the therapist's notations of the therapy sessions indicate that he or she is perplexed about a given case or appears to have more difficulty with certain cases, or if it seems that a certain type of client terminates prematurely, an opportunity is afforded the therapist to try to learn from such observations. In essence, the therapist looks for patterns and for possible cues in these instances that might indicate why some problems tend to arise or that suggest possible types of cases that are particularly troublesome for the therapist to handle. Such evaluations can alert the therapist to potential difficulties with comparable cases in the future and may also increase the therapist's sensitivity when working with such individuals, and this helps the therapist become more effective therapeutically.

Going over therapy notes, particularly when the therapy process is not going along as well as possible, provides the therapist with an opportunity to evaluate what may be occurring and to consider modifications in his or her approach. When therapy appears to be proceeding in a positive manner, the therapist is less likely to look over his or her notes and to ponder about the process of therapy. However, when little progress is being made, or when the therapist is aware that there are some indications of difficulties in the therapeutic relationship, it is important to take the time to evaluate the progress or lack of progress for the specific case. In trying to evaluate and understand the factors that may be affecting the process of therapy, the therapist may be able both to gain increased understanding of what is occurring and also to modify his or her therapeutic approach so as to change the course of therapy in a more positive direction. In some instances, such appraisal may give the therapist a bit more insight into how he or she reacts to certain events or to certain clients. In other instances, such a review may help the therapist to consider using a new procedure that might improve the current therapy.

For illustrative purposes, I refer to a couple of cases that I worked with in the past. In reviewing my therapy notes for the purpose of selecting a case to be used for my ABPP examination, I noted how differently I responded to the two clients whose cases I was considering for this purpose. One of the individuals tended to be quite negative and critical, and in response to this behavior I in turn was more verbally active and made comments that could be viewed as critical of the client. As I became more aware of my pattern of behavior and realized that I was behaving more in a defensive mode than in a therapeutic mode, I was able to change my view of the client and my behavior toward him. This change also led to an improved relationship in therapy and to a reduction in the client's critical behavior during the therapy hour. In the other case, my review of the therapy notes led me to believe that I was being too passive in therapy and that a more active stance was called for lest the therapy continue forever. Here again, it was my subjective judgment that the changes that I did undertake led to greater positive movement in therapy and in the eventual outcome.

REALISTIC SELF-APPRAISAL

Although in this chapter I have stressed the importance of attempting to evaluate one's therapeutic work and in using such appraisals as a means of self-learning, I warn the reader that this procedure should not be overdone. I strongly believe that one should try to learn from one's life experiences, and that this can be done in a meaningful and constructive manner. This is certainly manifested in that we prefer experienced people over nonexperienced to perform a variety of tasks ranging from surgery to plumbing to gardening. However, examining and evaluating one's experience, professional or otherwise, should not lead to undue introspection and self-criticism. What is desired is a process of self-learning and not either gratuitous self-adulation or morbid self-criticism. It is certainly possible to learn from one's experience in performing certain tasks, including the professional practice of psychotherapy. We can profit from evaluating earlier mistakes as well as later successes.

Our own experience as psychotherapists is undoubtedly the most important in evaluating the utility and efficacy of the procedures employed in our therapeutic work. Although we may not always be completely accurate in his or her appraisal of what is truly important in psychotherapy, still, our own experience is probably the most vivid and has the greatest impact. This is both understandable and reasonable according to most theories of personality. Yet, no true professional should practice in isolation and be unaware of significant developments and research in his or her particular field. Thus, in addition to the self-learning that is possible from the kind of self-appraisal described in this chapter, there are other opportunities for self-learning. Keeping up with the literature is one kind of professional and scientific learning that is familiar to all therapists, although it is essentially impossible to do so. The expansion of the field of psychotherapy, the proliferation of psychotherapeutic approaches, and the appearance of so many new journals and books each year is enough to overwhelm the scholar, let alone the busy practitioner. At the same time, there is a real danger in at least not making some attempt to be aware of new developments and research findings. To practice in one mold without inputs from the field from which one's practice is derived is to limit seriously the adequacy of that practice.

Most therapists have tried in various ways to keep abreast at least of some aspects of the developments in psychotherapy by receiving professional journals, attending professional meetings, and participating in psychotherapy workshops. All of these have some potential value in providing psychotherapists with new ideas and evaluations of existing procedures and techniques. The main problem in this connection is that the reading and professional contacts not be overly narrow and limited to one exclusive approach. Too much inbreeding is not desirable.

Chapter 9

Brief Therapy: An Appraisal and Summary

In the preceding pages I have tried to describe the process of brief psychotherapy as understood and practiced by one eclectic psychotherapist. The formulation and description of common factors as variables of importance in this process most likely distinguished this presentation from other treatises on brief psychotherapy. However, as has been pointed out, most forms of psychotherapy also appear to rely on common therapeutic factors although their conceptualizations and theories may differ. The comparative research literature on outcome in psychotherapy, which for the most part reveals little difference between various forms of psychotherapy, can be referred to in support of this statement (Garfield, 1983b; Lambert et al. 1986; Smith et al., 1980). In fact, it is desirable at this point to discuss in more detail the issue of the efficacy of psychotherapy generally and brief psychotherapy in particular. In doing so, I review some of the important research findings bearing on this issue. More comprehensive reviews are available in the previously cited references as well as in others yet to be mentioned.

Although practically all the psychotherapists with whom I have had contact have indicated or implied that their therapeutic work has been very successful, except when they have had a very difficult patient, I take their appraisals with a bit of skepticism. To say that a psychotherapist is highly ego-involved in his or her psychotherapeutic work is to state the case mildly. Although such involvement is necessary if one is to become an accomplished therapist, some degree of objectivity is also required. In the same way that a psychotherapist must maintain an objective stance toward his or her patient at the same time that he or she is highly empathic, the therapist must be objective in the evaluation of

143

his or her work. I discussed some ways of doing this in the previous chapter. It is also important for the therapist to be aware of the research findings related to his or her practice. This should provide a deeper perspective on the field as a whole as well as indicating potential problems and areas of difficulty.

Beginning with the development of psychoanalysis at the turn of the century and for many years thereafter, there were no truly systematic attempts at evaluating the effectiveness or outcome of psychotherapy. Within psychoanalysis, different factions developed based on differing views of personality and psychotherapy. Rarely, if ever, were theoretical or technical disagreements settled by recourse to any type of empirical data. Instead, appeals were made to the leader or to the established dogma of a given orientation. In the 1940s, however, critical discussions concerning the outcome of psychoanalytic therapy were reported by Oberndorf (1943) and by others (Oberndorf, Greenacre, & Kubie, 1948). These reports reflected concerns about evaluating the efficacy of psychoanalytic therapy, but no empirical studies were featured. The first noteworthy report claiming to evaluate the effects of psychotherapy was published by the British psychologist, Hans Eysenck, in 1952. As most readers probably know, Eysenck's report was exceedingly critical concerning the effectiveness of psychotherapy. According to his evaluation of 24 studies, psychoanalysis was judged to be considerably less effective than no therapy, and so-called eclectic psychotherapy only slightly less effective than no therapy. Eysenck's review stirred up considerable controversy regarding the efficacy of psychotherapy, which has persisted even to the present time. However, a considerable amount of research on outcome in psychotherapy has been conducted since the 1950s, and at least we are now better prepared to evaluate this issue. Also, the recent emphasis on accountability in psychotherapy has led to a greater focus on outcome research.

RESEARCH ON OUTCOME IN PSYCHOTHERAPY

The research literature on outcome in psychotherapy covers a wide spectrum in terms of therapists, clients, settings, outcome measures, type of therapy, and methods of analysis. The studies conducted also differ in terms of length of psychotherapy, although most of the studies, particularly the better designed ones, have been carried out on brief therapies. First, it is worth examining a brief summary of the major reviews of psychotherapy outcome in general. Then some specific studies of outcome in brief psychotherapy are discussed.

Although Eysenck followed his initial critical review on the effectiveness of psychotherapy (1952) with two equally critical reviews in 1961 and 1966, most of the later reviews tended to be more positive. Meltzoff and Kornreich (1970) reviewed 101 studies and concluded that psychotherapy actually was effective. They criticized Eysenck for omitting a number of studies that were favorable to psychotherapy. A year later, Bergin (1971) published a scholarly review in which he critically reanalyzed the data in Eysenck's 1952 review. He concluded that the effects of psychotherapy were modestly positive. Rachman, at that time a colleague of Eysenck, also published two reviews (1971, 1973) and agreed generally with Eysenck's evaluation and not with Bergin's. Except for the behavioral therapies, he did not find much research support for the effectiveness of psychotherapy.

A couple of years later, Luborsky, Singer, and Luborsky (1975), in their review of studies that met certain research criteria, reached a very positive conclusion, namely "that a high percentage of patients who go through any of these psychotherapies gain from them" (p. 1003). The review by Bergin and Lambert (1978) was an updating of Bergin's earlier review and was generally consistent with the conclusions drawn earlier.

In the latter part of the 1970s, a new methodology was applied to the evaluation of outcome in psychotherapy known as meta-analysis (Smith & Glass, 1977; Smith et al., 1980). This procedure essentially allows the researcher to analyze studies statistically in a way that is comparable to the analysis carried out on subjects in an individual study. One of the main benefits claimed for meta-analysis is that it reduces the potential bias of the individuals who conduct the literature reviews. No further discussion of this methodology is provided here. Those interested in this procedure can consult other references (Garfield, 1983a; Kazdin, 1986; Lambert et al., 1986). I simply refer to the findings reported by Smith et al. (1980) on their meta-analysis of 475 studies, the largest review of psychotherapy outcome ever published.

In this analysis, Smith and her colleagues found an average effect size for psychotherapy outcome that they considered to be large and significant. It was reported that 80% of the treated groups exceeded the means of the untreated groups. In many ways, this review was considered as the most favorable review of outcome in psychotherapy. Practitioners welcomed it, but others were at times highly critical (Garfield, 1983a, 1983b). The review by Rachman and Wilson (1980), for example, was quite critical of the Smith and Glass (1977) analysis as well as the reviews by Bergin (1971) and Luborsky et al. (1975).

In general, except for the reviews by Eysenck (1952, 1961, 1966), Rachman (1971), and Rachman and Wilson (1980), most of the reviews, including the more recent review of Lambert et al. (1986), have concluded that psychotherapy is effective, although the degree of effectiveness varies with the different reviewers. Clearly, not everyone is helped by psychotherapy and not everyone is helped to the same extent. There are differences in clients and therapists that also contribute to the types of outcome secured. Furthermore, as mentioned in chapter 2, despite the many different forms of psychotherapy, most reviews of research on outcome have generally found few significant differences between the different approaches.

Thus, although we can say, more often than not, that psychotherapy tends to produce positive results, it is difficult to make overly strong generalizations. As already noted, there are many variables that can influence outcome, and planning and carrying out a project to evaluate outcome in psychotherapy is a difficult and complicated matter. Consequently, although research evaluations of the efficacy of treatment are necessary from a social, scientific, and ethical point of view, it is important to evaluate the research studies in terms of their adequacy and relevance. Having reviewed some general appraisals of outcome in psychotherapy, I now examine some research findings pertaining more directly to brief psychotherapy.

EVALUATIONS OF BRIEF PSYCHOTHERAPY

I begin this discussion of the efficacy of brief psychotherapy by referring to some of the appraisals mentioned in several of the well-known reviews. For example, in the review by Luborsky et al. (1975), reference was made to eight controlled studies in which brief time-limited therapy was compared with time-unlimited therapy. In this comparison, time-limited therapy was found to be better in two studies, time-unlimited therapy was better in one comparison, and in the remaining five studies there were essentially no differences. The overall findings thus indicate that the results of brief time-limited therapy are at least as good as those of therapies that were longer and time-unlimited. In their meta-analytic review, Smith et al. (1980) also found no significant relationship between duration of therapy and outcome. Koss and Butcher (1986), in their recent review of research on brief psychotherapy, came to a similar conclusion: "In summary, comparative studies of brief psychotherapy offer little empirical evidence of differences in overall effectiveness between time-limited and -unlimited therapy or between alternate approaches to brief therapy" (p. 660).

On the basis of these reviews, it is fair to say that at the present time brief or time-limited psychotherapy appears to be as effective as therapy that continues for a longer time. The comparison therapies have varied in terms of time, but they have been longer, in some cases twice as long, as the time-limited therapy. Some therapists have commented that such comparisons should not be viewed as applying to long-term psychodynamic therapy, because the latter has not been one of the therapies compared. That is true, but in the absence of such studies, we cannot make any valid judgments of the effectiveness of the long-term psychodynamic therapy either.

I now turn to some specific studies of brief or time-limited psychotherapy. In one of the earliest studies, a group of 20 individuals who received time-unlimited client-centered therapy were compared with comparable clients who received client-centered time-limited therapy and with another group who received time-limited Adlerian therapy (Shlien et al., 1962). Both of the latter groups were limited to 20 sessions, whereas the time-unlimited group averaged 37 sessions. At both termination and at a subsequent follow-up, the two time-limited groups did at least as well as the group with unlimited time. Clearly, the time-limited therapy was more efficient than the therapy without such limits.

Another early study that is worth reporting here is the study by Muench (1965). Originally, Muench had proposed comparing time-unlimited therapy with therapy limited to eight sessions. However, the staff at the San Jose State College Counseling Center expressed concerns that this would be grossly unfair to the clients selected for the time-limited briefer therapy. Eventually a new design was accepted in which three groups would be studied and where the therapist was allowed to continue therapy beyond the time-limit if he felt it was desirable. The three therapy groups were: a short-term therapy to be terminated in less than eight sessions; a time-limited therapy with the clients told that therapy would be terminated at the 10th interview; and time-unlimited therapy that lasted for at least 20 sessions. Two objective measures were used to evaluate outcome. On one, there were no significant differences between the two groups; on the other, the two brief therapy groups did significantly better than the longer therapy group. What is particularly interesting about this study is that the results actually had an impact on practice. When the study was completed, the staff decided to utilize a time-limited brief approach as their standard method of psychotherapy.

The report of a large-scale brief psychotherapy program for children conducted at the Children's Psychiatric Center in Eatontown, New Jersey also deserves mention here (Leventhal & Weinberger, 1975). Although some clinical centers for children have utilized brief therapy in the past, relatively few evaluative studies have been conducted.

The Children's Psychiatric Center had functioned as a traditional "long-term, personality-reconstruction, team treatment of family members seen individually. Gradually, in response to staff discomfort with this model's level of efficiency and effectiveness, a brief therapy program was developed that totally reversed the former rationale and procedure" (Leventhal & Weinberger, 1975, p. 120). The changes made were quite remarkable. The formal pretreatment diagnostic evaluations were eliminated, as was the team approach. Instead, all clients were assigned immediately into a brief therapy period of 6 weeks, with a modal number of two sessions per week. The length of treatment was told to the family prior to the beginning of treatment, and the family was assigned as a unit to one therapist who had the total responsibility for managing the case. At the end of the 6-week period, the family and therapist evaluated the progress and decided if additional treatment was required. If the latter was the decision, additional therapy was offered.

The aforementioned program emphasizes competence and views the client as having problems in living. The self, as an organized set of beliefs about one's abilities, becomes the focus of the therapy. In a related manner, attention is focused on problem areas (rather than total personality factors), on the here-and-now, and on volitional aspects and strengths in client functioning. The stated goals of this form of brief psychotherapy "are to reduce discrepancies, help clients view themselves and others more realistically, act more congruently with attainable goals, and feel more in control of their own lives" (Leventhal & Weinberger, 1975, p. 121).

In the initial 4 years of this program, over 1,700 families were seen, and they were evaluated in terms of five different criteria including dispositions, readmissions, and several rating scales completed by therapists and parents. There is no need here to go into a description of the procedures and all of the analyses performed. In general, the occurrences of positive outcome are comparable to those reported for longer-term therapies, 66% to 83%, depending on the measure used. Also, "One of the most striking findings was the small number of drop-outs" (Leventhal & Weinberger, 1975, p. 123). Less than 10% of the cases that only received brief therapy were readmitted as cases, which compares quite favorably with reports of those seeking therapy who have had previous therapy (Sloane et al., 1975).

In the studies and reviews discussed thus far, the research findings indicate some effectiveness for psychotherapy in general as compared with no treatment or comparable types of control groups, and also that brief psychotherapies appear to do at least as well as the longer-term psychotherapies to which they have been compared. There are also a few important studies comparing different forms of psychotherapy that are of interest. The study by Sloane and his colleagues (1975) is probably so well known that this report can be relatively brief.

In the Sloane study, psychoanalytically oriented brief therapy was compared with behavior therapy. Both forms of therapy were limited to a 4-month period of weekly sessions and were also compared with a wait-list control group. The mean number of sessions was 13.2 for the behavior therapy and 14.2 for the psychoanalytically oriented therapy. The therapists were well known and experienced, and the patients' symptoms on average were considered to be moderately severe. The focus for evaluation was on the three major complaints of the clients, although a number of outcome measures were used. In general, "a patient treated by behavior therapy and psychotherapy showed significantly greater reduction in the severity of their target symptoms than did patients on the wait-list control" (Sloane et al., 1975, p. 94). In addition, there were no significant differences between the two different forms of therapy.

Another extremely important study of brief psychotherapy is the Collaborative Study of the Treatment of Depression sponsored and coordinated by the National Institute of Mental Health under the leadership of Irene Elkin (Elkin et al., 1985). This large-scale study, conducted at three collaborating medical centers and representing the state of the art in psychotherapy research, has just been completed but published reports are not yet available. However, presentations have been made at several professional meetings, and the overall results obtained at the end of treatment can be mentioned here.

In this study, depressed patients were assigned to one of four treatments. Two of the treatments were Beck's (1979) cognitive therapy and the interpersonal therapy developed by Klerman, Weissman and their colleagues (Klerman et al., 1984). These two psychotherapies were compared with imipramine, a well-known pharmacological treatment for depression, and with a pill-placebo plus clinical management treatment condition. The latter was considered as a control for the imipramine condition, which also included clinical management. It should be emphasized that the two pharmacological treatments were more than just the dispensing of pills. The patients who received these treatments also saw their therapists weekly for the 16 weeks allocated for each of the treatments and received support and encouragement from them.

All of the therapists were highly selected clinical psychologists or psychiatrists who, in addition to their own previous professional training and experience, received specific training and supervision for the therapy they performed in this investigation. Specific therapy manuals were developed for each of the therapies. A variety of measures were used to evaluate outcome, but only a few of the main findings are mentioned here. The findings are complex and refer to evaluations made at the end of treatment. However, data have also been secured from follow-up evaluations at 6 months, 12 months, and 18 months. These data, when fully analyzed, will augment the post-treatment data and allow for a more definitive appraisal of treatment efficacy.

The preliminary results secured at the end of treatment showed no significant differences between either of the psychotherapies and imipramine or between the two psychotherapies in reduction of depressive symptoms or in overall functioning. All of the three main treatments as well as the pill-placebo plus clinical management condition secured significant reductions in depressive symptomatology. Although the patients in the three treatment groups consistently secured better outcomes than the patients in the so-called placebo group, the differences for the most part did not reach statistical significance. It is important to remember, however, that the latter group of patients were seen by experienced psychiatrists on a regular weekly basis, as indicated earlier.

In general, the findings secured from the collaborative study are congruent with those secured from other comparable studies. A few additional results also merit mention. Patients considered severely depressed (a score of 20 or more on the Hamilton Rating Scale for Depression), who received interpersonal psychotherapy or imipramine, secured significantly lower scores than the placebo plus clinical management group at the end of treatment. Although this was not true for the cognitive behavioral therapy group, the results for this therapy were quite variable across the three participating research centers, and we must await the final results and analyses before drawing any conclusions.

There is one other set of results that I mention before concluding this brief report of the collaborative study. Actually, the main impetus for conducting the study was to compare the general and specific effectiveness of the two rather well-known psychotherapies for depression. Although both were developed for the treatment of depression, they were two very different approaches that could be reliably differentiated. Consequently, it was hypothesized that some specific differential outcomes would be secured for the two psychotherapies, for example, a greater improvement in social adjustment for patients receiving interpersonal psychotherapy and a comparable improvement in cognitive functioning for the patients receiving cognitive behavioral therapy. In general, however, such specific differential effects were not secured. Rather, improvement occurred for both groups across a wide range of outcome measures. Thus, despite the fact that the two psychotherapies clearly differ in theoretical orientation and procedures, their outcomes were essentially similar, even when specific types of outcomes assumed to be related to the therapies in question were evaluated.

These results resemble the results secured in the Sloane et al. (1975) study of psychoanalytically oriented brief therapy and behavior therapy discussed earlier. Not only were there no significant differences between these two different forms of psychotherapy, but when the successful patients were asked to name the factors they believed were responsible for their improvement, the patients from both groups gave the same type of responses. The following quotations from the study by Sloane et al. (1975) clearly illustrate this interesting finding:

> The following items were each termed "extremely important" or "very important" by at least 70 percent of successful patients in both groups:
> 1. The personality of your doctor.
> 2. His helping you to understand your problem.
> 3. Encouraging you gradually to practice facing the things that bother you.
> 4. Being able to talk to an understanding person.
> 5. Helping you to understand yourself. (p. 206)

> Nearly all these items can be classified as "encouragement, advice, or reassurance," factors common to both behavior therapy and psychotherapy. None of the items regarded as very important by the majority of either group of patients describes techniques specific to one therapy. . . . Most noticeable is the great overlap between the two groups, suggesting that, at least from the patient's point of view, the effectiveness of treatment was due to factors common to both therapies rather than to any particular theoretical orientation or techniques. (p. 207)

This view obviously is congruent with my viewpoint. There is no need or justification to overemphasize this view. The only point to be stressed is that this conceptualization of the importance of common therapeutic factors or variables in psychotherapy appears to have support from empirical studies evaluating outcome in psychotherapy. Even if some therapists are reluctant to give much credence or emphasis to this view, they can at least note that the research findings presented do lend some fairly clear support for the efficacy of brief psychotherapy.

SOME BASIC CONSIDERATIONS

Before offering final comments on brief psychotherapy, it is worthwhile to emphasize once more some of the basic features and objectives of brief psychotherapy. Above all, brief therapy is problem centered and has a specific goal—to help the client overcome the current problem and to be able (as much as possible) to meet the requirements of daily living.

Although various approaches to brief psychotherapy may conceptualize what is wrong with the client in very different ways (Budman, 1981), the therapist must always keep in mind that it is the client's problem that should determine the treatment and be its focus.

Therapists must be sensitive to some general features that characterize most clients who seek out psychotherapeutic help. They can be characterized as experiencing some degree of hopelessness or demoralization, as suffering from low self-esteem, and as perceiving their life situation as well as their own selves in an overly critical or negative manner. Clearly, these general attributes of the client need to be modified if the client is to be helped by means of psychotherapy. These, again, are general characteristics that can be noted in practically all clients regardless of their specific problems, complaints, or clinical diagnoses.

Consequently, although the focus of therapy may center around the specific problem for which the patient seeks help, the therapist also needs to devote attention to these important general characteristics. Being given an appointment, being accepted for psychotherapy, and being informed that brief psychotherapy is likely to be helpful are all factors that begin to signal hope to the patient and to lessen his or her feelings of isolation and demoralization. Many individuals have remarked that simply making an appointment with a therapist has made them feel better. It is important to be aware of this, but it is also important to remember that such feelings need to be followed by more specific activities that provide concrete evidence of therapeutic progress.

Therapy can increase the client's self-esteem in several different ways. Attempts at cognitive restructuring, in which the therapist helps the client to see him or herself in a more realistic and positive manner, is one method. The therapist's genuine and sincere regard for the client is another. Closely related to this is the positive reinforcement that the therapist provides at various times for the client's performance during therapy. Perhaps most important, however, is the sense of adequacy or mastery that the client secures from being able to overcome his or her difficulties and to improve his or her daily life situation. The old adage, nothing succeeds like success, is also applicable to psychotherapy. Successful performance has powerful consequences. It conveys to the client that he or she does have control over his or her life.

If the therapist conveys competence, sincerity, and interest in the client's welfare and is perceived as a person whom the client can trust, the chances for a successful therapeutic outcome are greatly enhanced. The personal qualities of the psychotherapist play a significant role in the therapeutic process and in the type of outcome that is eventually secured, as already noted. They are aspects of therapy to which clients respond very early in therapy, and may determine whether or not a client will continue in therapy. These statements pertain to all forms of psychotherapy regardless of theoretical orientation.

Because I have mentioned the personal qualities of the psychotherapist, I also refer to a few other related matters that are of some importance. The therapist must be a person of integrity and with a high sense of moral values. The personal values of the patient must be respected unless the therapist is dealing with a clearly amoral or criminal individual. Although the patient may in some fashion model him or herself after the therapist and take on some of the therapist's values, this should be a free decision of the patient and not the result of indoctrination.

Although outcome in psychotherapy appears to be influenced in a significant manner by the personality of the therapist, this is not to say that this is all there is to psychotherapy. Skill in the use of therapeutic procedures and techniques is also important. There have at times been arguments and discussions about the relative importance of the therapist's personality and therapeutic techniques as the factors responsible for positive outcome in psychotherapy. To me, this is like arguing as to what is more important for life, air or water? Without question, both are essential for life to exist. In the same way, the therapist's personal qualities and skill in using the techniques and procedures of psychotherapy are both essential for positive therapeutic results. They interact and compliment each other as therapy proceeds. The different approaches to psychotherapy may appear to emphasize one over the other in their formal presentations. However, what therapists do in therapy and how they actually conduct their therapeutic efforts may differ from the formal descriptions of the therapies.

I would prefer to emphasize the skill of the therapist rather than to focus on techniques. Choosing the appropriate time to respond to the client's statements and responding in an effective manner are not necessarily techniques of therapy, but they do reveal the relative skill of the therapist. In a similar way, although exposure may be viewed as a technique of behavioral therapy, when to use it in therapy and how to use it are not automatic affairs. The skill of the therapist, which includes the therapist's ability to judge and evaluate the particular client and the particular situation is also involved in the use of such procedures. Unfortunately, and perhaps surprisingly, there have been very few studies evaluating the comparative skills of psychotherapists. Despite this paucity of systematic efforts to evaluate therapeutic skill, most psychotherapists and most training supervisors will tell you that therapists do indeed differ in their skills and effectiveness.

As indicated previously, the conscientious therapist can attempt to evaluate and improve his or her performance in psychotherapy. It is well to keep in mind that not all psychological or mental disorders can be treated effectively by means of psychotherapy, brief or otherwise. It is also important to realize that therapists, as individuals, may work more effectively with some types of clients than with others, and there are some clients with whom they rarely succeed. Therapists usually start their careers with what sometimes appears as a missionary zeal combined with some strands of anxiety. They are ready to save suffering humanity, although doubts crop up from time to time. However, as therapists gain in experience and maturity and as they make some attempts to evaluate their own work, they can more readily gauge the limits of their effectiveness and the types of cases that they are most competent to handle. Thus, as mentioned earlier, the skilled therapist decides if the problem presented is a suitable one for psychotherapy, appraises the potential client in terms of the latter's desire to collaborate in therapy, and then decides if he or she feels able to work with this individual. If the responses to these three items are positive, the therapist, on the basis of the information supplied by the client (or others) and his or her observation of the client's behavior, can begin to formulate possible plans for conducting the therapy.

BRIEF PSYCHOTHERAPY IN PERSPECTIVE

In the preceding pages, I have presented my views about brief psychotherapy. As indicated, the perspective has been an eclectic one and reference has been made to views and procedures drawn from a variety of sources. The presentation has also been general, in that the approach is deemed applicable to a number of psychological problems that involve feelings of inadequacy, anxiety, and depression. There are also a number of therapeutic approaches that have been developed as brief treatments for specific disorders or problems such as depression, anxiety reaction, agoraphobia, bulimia, assertiveness, and some others. In fact, a number of the books in the present Guidebook Series are of this type. If the therapist's practice is limited to treating one specific disorder, then perhaps a more specialized approach is preferred. However, if the therapist's practice is more general and includes working with a variety of different cases, a more general treatise of the present type may be useful. Therapists, of course, are not limited to relying on only one source of information or to using one approach. An advantage of an eclectic approach is that the therapist can use whatever procedures or theories appear relevant and potentially useful when working with different individuals.

As discussed in chapter 1, brief forms of psychotherapy have become quite popular in recent years. A variety of factors undoubtedly have played a role in this development, and unless some very significant changes in our society take place, brief forms of psychotherapy will continue to be popular. A number of supposedly different forms of brief psychotherapy have been developed. In fact, the number of different psychodynamic forms of brief psychotherapy is surprising. Koss and Butcher (1986), in their comprehensive review of research on brief psychotherapy, noted that the psychodynamic forms of brief psychotherapy are the most numerous and listed over 20 different approaches or types. In his book on forms of brief therapy, Budman (1981) also devoted most of the chapters to presentations of psychodynamic forms of brief psychotherapy.

This variability of psychotherapeutic approaches is indeed an interesting phenomenon, and, as mentioned earlier, is one that has intrigued me for some time. I tend to favor the view that most, if not all, forms of psychotherapy essentially rely to a great extent on common factors for whatever positive outcomes are secured. However, not everyone agrees with this view. An interesting and contrary view is presented by White, Burke, and Havens (1981). These authors adapted various developmental approaches to indicate five specific stages of development. They suggested that certain specific types of brief psychotherapy are each uniquely suited for the different stages of development. For example, Mann's (1973) approach, which emphasized conflicts of separations individuation, was judged to be an ideal therapy for adolescents who typically have such conflicts. Sifneos' (1981) approach, on the other hand, which focuses on oedipal problems, was seen as a particularly appropriate therapy for clients in early adulthood. In a similar manner, the approaches of Alexander and French (1946) and some others were considered to be most efficacious for adult clients in later developmental stages.

Although the formulation just presented has a certain appeal based on the rationale of differential treatment for individuals with supposedly different problems, I have difficulty in accepting it. I doubt that all individuals within a certain age range have exactly the same underlying or symptomatic problems when they seek out therapy. Furthermore, in recent years a number of therapies have been developed by cognitive-behavioral therapists for such problems as depression, phobic behaviors, sexual difficulties, and the like. Do these different approaches, therefore, simply reflect the theoretical differences between psychodynamic and cognitive-behavioral orientations to therapy? To a great extent they do, although it must be admitted that the behaviorally oriented therapists have provided more empirical evidence in support of their views, and this is of some significance. We must await the results of additional research before any definite conclusions can be reached.

Having stated the usual disclaimer that further research is needed, I state again that research productivity and the quality of the research on brief psychotherapy has increased steadily over the past 25 years. Furthermore, the recent development of treatment manuals has featured brief therapies almost exclusively. Along with the time limits imposed by most third-party payers and the recent emphasis on accountability, these developments would appear to support the dominance of brief psychotherapy over the longer forms of psychotherapy. Most of the psychotherapy that is conducted in the United States, at least, is brief therapy, and there is no basis for expecting any change in the immediate future. There are still opportunities for those individuals who want to enter psychoanalysis or receive some other type of long-term psychotherapy as a means of personal self-exploration in terms of a specific theory of personality. However, such therapy is clearly for the very few who desire such an experience and can afford to pay for it. For the rest of the population, brief psychotherapy remains the treatment of choice.

Before concluding this final chapter, I mention one other recent development in the field of psychotherapy that, although claiming only a few adherents, is of possible importance. I refer to the recent movement for rapprochement and integration in psychotherapy among a number of outstanding psychotherapists. Particularly interesting is that this movement has featured behavior therapists and analytically oriented psychotherapists, two unlikely collaborators. A number of papers and books have been published pertaining to integration in psychotherapy, and I refer to them briefly here.

Early articles suggesting some combination and integration of psychodynamic and behavioral procedures were published by Marmor in 1971 and by Feather and Rhodes in 1972. The article by Marmor, for example, was titled, "Dynamic psychotherapy and behavior therapy. Are they irreconcilable?" A few years later, Paul Wachtel (1977) published his book, *Psychoanalysis and Behavior Therapy*. Wachtel, an analytically oriented therapist, described how he had added behavioral techniques to his therapeutic approach.

This broadened view of psychotherapy on the part of some dynamically oriented therapists was soon matched by similar manifestations on the part of behavioral and cognitive therapists, particularly Marvin Goldfried. Goldfried published an important article in the *American Psychologist* (1980) and also edited a volume containing a number of articles illustrating converging themes in psychotherapy (Goldfried, 1982). In 1984, the Society for the Exploration of Psychotherapy Integration, or SEPI, was formed, and annual meetings have been held since then. The leaders of this new organization include such well-known individuals as Marvin Goldfried, Paul Wachtel, Aaron T. Beck, Allen Bergin, Hans Strupp, Gerald Davison, Merton Gill, Alan Gurman, and Donald Meichenbaum among others—certainly a diverse group.

Although this movement toward integration may overlap with eclecticism in psychotherapy, it is somewhat distinct. The main goals of the integrationists are to integrate two or more orientations in some kind of systematic or theoretical manner. As I have read some of their individual papers, it seems to me as if they have not given up their original theoretical identifications. Nevertheless, in recognizing that the use of more than one approach or form of psychotherapy seems desirable, these individuals also reveal a broadened approach that at least resembles those of eclectic psychotherapists. I tend to combine integration and eclecticism as one movement in psychotherapy that favors breadth in therapy and is opposed to the proliferation of psychotherapeutic approaches. That I am not alone in combining these two emphases is indicated by the current appearance of the *Journal of Integrative and Eclectic Psychotherapy,* edited by John Norcross and published by Brunner/ Mazel. Which one of these opposite movements (integration and eclecticism or proliferation) will have the greatest impact on the field in the future is difficult to predict. Because I am not a completely unbiased observer in this instance, my own observations and predictions must be taken "with a grain of salt."

My own view is that, in the long run, the individuals who strive for an integrative eclecticism are likely to have the greatest influence on future developments in psychotherapy. The leaders of this movement are outstanding psychotherapists who have made important contributions to psychotherapy and who may provide significant new systematizations of the field. Many of these individuals are research oriented, and their work is thus more likely to be evaluated than is true of most new forms of psychotherapy. In the current climate of accountability, this is an important aspect. As more systematic and effective forms of psychotherapy make their appearance, unproven and less effective forms of therapy will gradually disappear. This has been the history of medical treatments, and I am confident it will also be true for psychotherapy, including of course, brief psychotherapy.

References

Affleck, D. C., & Garfield, S. L. (1961). Predictive judgments of therapists and duration of stay in psychotherapy. *Journal of Clinical Psychology, 17,* 134–137.

Alexander, F. (1944). The brief psychotherapy council and its outlook. *Psychosomatic Medicine, Proceedings of the Second Brief Psychotherapy Council.* Chicago: Institute for Psychoanalysis, 1–4.

Alexander, F., & French, T. M. (1946). *Psychoanalytic therapy. Principles and application.* New York: Ronald Press.

Avnet, H. H. (1965). How effective is short-term therapy? In L. R. Wolberg (Ed.), *Short-term psychotherapy* (pp. 7–22). New York: Grune & Stratton.

Bandura, A., Blancard, E. B., & Ritter, B. (1969). The relative efficacy of desensitization and modeling approaches for inducing behavioral, affective, and attitudinal change. *Journal of Personality and Social Psychology, 13,* 173–199.

Bandura, A., Jeffrey, R. W., & Wright, C. L. (1974). Efficacy of participant modeling as a function of response induction aids. *Journal of Abnormal Psychology, 83,* 56–64.

Beck, A. T. (1976). *Cognitive therapy and the emotional disorders.* New York: International Universities Press.

Beck, A. T., Rush, A. J., Shaw, B. F., & Emery, G. (1979). *Cognitive therapy of depression: A treatment manual.* New York: Guilford.

Beck, A. T., Ward, C. H., Mendelson, M., Mock, J. E., & Erbaugh, J. K. (1961). An inventory for measuring depression. *Archives of General Psychiatry, 4,* 561–571.

Bellak, L., & Small, L., (1965). *Emergency psychotherapy and brief psychotherapy.* New York: Grune and Stratton.

Bennet, M. J., & Wisneski, M. J. (1979). Continuous psychotherapy within an HMO. *American Journal of Psychiatry, 136,* 1283–1287.

Bergin, A. E. (1971). The evaluation of therapeutic outcomes. In A. E. Bergin and S. L. Garfield (Eds.), *Handbook of psychotherapy and behavior change* (pp. 217–270). New York: Wiley.

Bergin, A. E., & Lambert, M. J. (1978). The evaluation of therapeutic outcomes. In S. L. Garfield & A. E. Bergin (Eds.), *Handbook of psychotherapy and behavior change* (2nd ed., pp. 139–190). New York: Wiley.

Berrigan, L. P., & Garfield, S. L. (1981). Relationship of missed psychotherapy appointments to premature termination and social class. *The British Journal of Clinical Psychology, 20,* 239–242.

Beutler, L. E. (1983). *Eclectic psychotherapy. A systematic approach.* New York: Pergamon Press.

Beutler, L. E., Crago, M., & Arizmendi, T. G. (1986). Research on therapist variables in psychotherapy. In S. L. Garfield & A. E. Bergin (Eds.), (3rd ed., pp. 257–310). *Handbook of psychotherapy and behavior change.* New York: Wiley.

Budman, S. H. (Ed.). (1981). *Forms of brief therapy.* New York: Guilford.

Budman, S. H., & Gurman, A. S. (1983). The practice of brief psychotherapy. *Professional Psychology: Research and Practice. 14,* 277–292.

Butcher, J. N., & Koss, M. P. (1978). Research on brief and crisis-oriented psychotherapies. In S. L. Garfield & A. E. Bergin (Eds.), (2nd ed., pp. 725–768). *Handbook of psychotherapy and behavior change.* New York: Wiley.

Colby, K. M. (1951). *A primer for psychotherapists.* New York: Ronald Press.

DeRubeis, R. J., Hollon, S. E., Evans, M. D., & Bemis, K. M. (1982). Can psychotherapies for depression be discriminated? A systematic investigation of cognitive therapy and interpersonal therapy. *Journal of Consulting and Clinical Psychology, 50,* 744–756.

Deutsch, C. J. (1984). Self-reported sources of stress among psychotherapists. *Professional Psychology: Research and Practice, 15,* 833–845.

Elkin, I., Parloff, M. B., Hadley, S. W., & Autry, J. H. (1985). NIMH treatment of depression collaborative research program. *Archives of General Psychiatry, 42,* 305–316.

Ellis, A. (1962). *Reason and emotion in psychotherapy.* New York: Lyle Stuart.

Ellis, A. (1985). *Overcoming resistance. Rational-Emotive therapy with difficult clients.* New York: Springer.

Emmelkamp, P. M. G. (1986). Behavior therapy with adults. In S. L. Garfield & A. E. Bergin (Eds.), (3rd ed., pp. 385–442). *Handbook of psychotherapy and behavior change.* New York: Wiley.

Erdwins, C. F. (1975). *A comparison of three behavior modification procedures including systematic desensitization and vicarious modeling.* Unpublished Doctoral Dissertation, Washington University, St. Louis, MO.

Eysenck, H. J. (1952). The effects of psychotherapy: An evaluation. *Journal of Consulting Psychology, 16,* 319–324.

Eysenck, H. J. (1961). The effects of psychotherapy. In H. J. Eysenck (Ed.), (pp. 697–725). *Handbook of abnormal psychology.* New York: Basic Books.

Eysenck, H. J. (1966). *The effects of psychotherapy.* New York: International Science Press.

Feather, B. W., & Rhoades, J. M. (1972). Psychodynamic behavior therapy. I. Theory and rationale. *Archives of General Psychiatry, 26,* 496–502.

Ferenczi, S., & Rank, O. (1925). *The development of psychoanalysis.* New York: Nervous and Mental Disease Monograph, No. 40.

Frank, J. D. (1971). Therapeutic factors in psychotherapy. *American Journal of Psychotherapy, 25,* 350–361.

Franks, C. M. (Ed.) (1969). *Behavior therapy: Appraisal and status.* New York: McGraw-Hill.

Frohman, B. S. (1948). *Brief psychotherapy.* Philadelphia: Lea and Febiger.

Garfield, S. L. (1957). *Introductory clinical psychology.* New York: Macmillan.

Garfield, S. L. (1974). *Clinical psychology. The study of personality and behavior.* Chicago, IL.: Aldine

Garfield, S. L. (1980). *Psychotherapy. An eclectic approach.* New York: Wiley.

Garfield. S. L. (1983a). Meta-analysis and psychotherapy: Introduction to special section. *Journal of Consulting and Clinical Psychology, 51,* 3.

Garfield, S. L. (1983b). The effectiveness of psychotherapy: The perennial controversy. *Professional Psychology, 14,* 35–43.

Garfield, S. L. (1986). Research on client variables in psychotherapy. In S. L. Garfield and A. E. Bergin, (Eds.), (3rd ed., pp. 213–256). *Handbook of psychotherapy and behavior change.* New York: Wiley.

Garfield, S. L., & Affleck, D. C. (1961). Therapist's judgments concerning patients considered for psychotherapy. *Journal of Consulting Psychology, 25,* 505–509.

Garfield, S. L., Affleck, D. C., & Muffley, R. A. (1963). A study of psychotherapy interaction and continuation in psychotherapy. *Journal of Clinical Psychology, 19,* 473–478.

Garfield, S. L., & Kurtz, R. (1976). Clinical psychologists in the 1970s. *American Psychologist, 31,* 1–9.

Garfield, S. L., & Kurtz, R. (1977). A study of eclectic views. *Journal of Consulting and Clinical Psychology, 45,* 78–83.

Garfield, S. L., & Kurz, M. (1952). Evaluation of treatment and related procedures in 1216 cases referred to a mental hygiene clinic. *Psychiatric Quarterly, 26,* 414–424.

Garfield, S. L., Prager, R. A., & Bergin, A. E. (1971). Evaluation of outcome in psychotherapy. *Journal of Consulting and Clinical Psychology, 37,* 307–313.

Garfield, S. L., & Wolpin, M. (1963). Expectations regarding psychotherapy. *Journal of Nervous and Mental Disease, 137,* 353–362.

Gelder, M. G., Bancroft, J. H. J., Gath, D. H., Johnston, D. W., Mathews, F. M., & Shaw, P. M. (1973). Specific and non-specific factors in behavior therapy. *The British Journal of Psychiatry, 123,* 445–462.

Glad, D. D. (1959). *Operational values in psychotherapy.* New York: Oxford University Press.

Goldfried, M. R. (1980). Toward the delineation of therapeutic change principles. *American Psychologist, 35,* 991–999.

Goldfried, M. R. (Ed.). (1982). *Converging themes in psychotherapy.* New York: Springer.

Goldfried, M. R., & Trier, C. S. (1974). Effectiveness of relaxation as an active coping skill. *Journal of Abnormal Psychology, 83,* 348–355.

Gomes-Schwartz, B. (1978). Effective ingredients in psychotherapy: Predictions of outcome from process variables. *Journal of Consulting and Clinical Psychology, 46,* 1023–1035.

Harris, M. R., Kalis, B., and Freeman, E. (1963). Precipitating stress: An approach to brief therapy. *American Journal of Psychotherapy, 17,* 465–471.

Harris, M. R., Kalis, B. L., & Freeman, E. H. (1964). An approach to short-term psychotherapy. *Mind, 2,* 198–206.

Haskell, D., Pugatch, D., & McNair, D. M. (1969). Time-limited psychotherapy for whom. *Archives of General Psychiatry, 21,* 546–552.

Herink, R. (Ed.). (1980). *The psychotherapy handbook. The A to Z guide to more than 250 different therapies in use today.* New York: New American Library.

Herzberg, A. (1946). *Active psychotherapy.* New York: Grune & Stratton.

Horenstein, D., Houston, B. K., & Holmes, D. S. (1973). Clients', therapists' and judges' evaluation of psychotherapy. *Counseling Psychology, 20,* 149–150.

Howard, G. S., Nance, D. W., & Myers, P. (1987). *Adaptive counseling and therapy.* San Francisco: Jossey-Bass.

Howard, K. I., Kopata, S. M., Krause, M. S., & Orlinsky, D. E. (1986). The dose-effect relationship in psychotherapy. *American Psychologist, 41,* 159–164.

Ivey, A. E., & Authier, J. (1978). *Microcounseling* (2nd ed.). Springfield, IL: Charles C. Thomas.

Jacobson, G. F. (1965). Crisis theory and treatment strategy: Some sociocultural and psychodynamic considerations. *The Journal of Nervous and Mental Disease, 141,* 209–218.

Joint Commission on Mental Illness and Health (1961). *Action for mental health.* New York: Basic Books.

Jourard, S. (1971). *Self-Disclosure.* New York: Wiley.

Kalis, B. L., Freeman, E. H., & Harris, M. R. (1964). Influence of previous help-seeking experiences on applications for psychotherapy. *Mental Hygiene, 48,* 267–272.

Kazdin, A. E. (1986). Comparative outcome studies of psychotherapy: Methodological issues and strategies. *Journal of Consulting and Clinical Psychology, 54,* 95–105.

Kelly, E. L. (1961). Clinical Psychology (1960): Report of survey findings. *American*

Psychological Association, Division of Clinical Psychology Newsletter, 14, (1), 1–11.

Klein, M. H., Dittman, A. T., Parloff, M. B., & Gill, M. M. (1969). Behavior therapy: Observations and reflections. *Journal of Consulting and Clinical Psychology, 33,* 259–266.

Klerman, G. L., Weissman, M. M., Rounsaville, B. J., & Chevron, E. S. (1984). *Interpersonal psychotherapy of depression (IPT).* New York: Basic Books.

Koss, M. P. (1979). Length of psychotherapy for clients seen in private practice. *Journal of Consulting and Clinical Psychology, 47,* 210–212.

Koss, M. P., & Butcher, J. N. (1986). Research on brief psychotherapy. In S. L. Garfield and A. E. Bergin (Eds.), (3rd ed., pp. 627–670). *Handbook of psychotherapy and behavior change.* New York: Wiley.

Lambert, M. J., Shapiro, D. A., & Bergin, A. E. (1986). The effectiveness of psychotherapy. In S. L. Garfield & A. E. Bergin (Eds.) (3rd ed., pp. 157–212). *Handbook of psychotherapy and behavior change.* New York: Wiley.

Levine, M. (1948). *Psychotherapy in medical practice.* New York: Macmillan.

Leventhal, T., & Weinberger, G. (1975). Evaluation of a large-scale brief therapy program for children. *American Journal of Orthopsychiatry, 45,* 119–133.

Lewinsohn, P. M., & Hoberman, H. M. (1982). Behavioral and cognitive approaches. In E. S. Paykel (Ed.), (pp. 338–345). *Handbook of affective disorders.* Edinburgh: Churchill Livingstone.

Lieberman, M. A., Yalom, I. D., & Miles, M. B. (1973). *Encounter groups: First facts.* New York: Basic Books.

Luborsky, L. (1984). *Principles of psychoanalytic psychotherapy: A manual for supportive-expressive treatment.* New York: Basic Books.

Luborsky, L., Crits-Christoph, P., Alexander, L., Margolis, M., & Cohen, M. (1983). Two helping alliance methods of predicting outcomes of psychotherapy. *Journal of Nervous and Mental Disease, 171,* 480–491.

Luborsky, L., Singer, B., & Luborsky, L. (1975). Comparative studies of psychotherapy. Is it true that "Everyone has won and all must have prizes"? *Archives of General Psychiatry, 32,* 995–1007.

Malan, D. H. (1963). *A study of brief psychotherapy.* New York: Plenum Press.

Malan, D. H. (1976). *Toward the validation of dynamic psychotherapy.* New York: Plenum Press.

Mann, J. (1973). *Time-limited psychotherapy.* Cambridge, MA: Harvard University Press.

Mann, J. (1981). The core of time-limited psychotherapy. In S. H. Budman (Ed.), (pp 25–43). *Forms of brief therapy.* New York: Guilford.

Marmor, J. (1971). Dynamic psychotherapy and behavior therapy. Are they irreconcilable? *Archives of General Psychiatry, 24,* 22–28.

Masters, W. H., & Johnson, V. E. (1970). *Human sexual inadequacy.* Boston: Little, Brown & Co.

Mathews, A. M., Gelder, M. G., & Johnston, D. W. (1981). *Agoraphobia. Nature and treatment.* London: Tavistock Publications.

Mathews, A. M., Johnston, D. W., Shaw, P. M., & Gelder, M. G. (1974). Process variables and the prediction of outcome in behavior therapy. *The British Journal of Psychiatry, 125,* 256–264.

Meltzoff, J., & Kornreich, M. (1970). *Research in psychotherapy.* New York: Atherton Press.

Mintz, J. (1981). Measuring outcome in psychodynamic psychotherapy: Psychodynamic vs. symptomatic assessment. *Archives of General Psychiatry, 38,* 503–506.

Muench, G. A. (1965). An investigation of the efficacy of time-limited psychotherapy. *Journal of Counseling Psychology, 12,* 294–299.

Murray, E. J. (1956). A content-analysis method for studying psychotherapy. *Psychological Monographs, 70,* (13, Serial No. 420).

Norcross, J. C. (Ed.). (1986). *Handbook of eclectic psychotherapy.* New York: Brunner/Mazel.

Oberndorf, C. P. (1943). Results of psychoanalytic therapy. *International Journal of Psychoanalysis, 24,* 107–114.

Oberndorf, C. P., Greenacre, P., & Kubie, L. (1948). Symposium on the evaluation of therapeutic results. *International Journal of Psychoanalysis, 29,* 7–33.

O'Leary, K. D., & Wilson, G. T. (1987). *Behavior therapy. Application and outcome* (2nd ed.). Englewood Cliffs, NJ: Prentice-Hall.

O'Malley, S. S., Suh, C. S., & Strupp, H. H. (1983). The Vanderbilt Psychotherapy Process Scale: A report on the scale development and a process-outcome study. *Journal of Consulting and Clinical Psychology, 51,* 581–586.

Paykel, E. S. (Ed.). (1982). *Handbook of affective disorders.* Edinburgh: Churchill Livingstone.

Pryzwansky, W. B., & Wendt, R. N. (1987). *Psychology as a profession. Foundations of practice.* New York: Pergamon Press.

Rachman, S. (1971). *The effects of psychotherapy.* Oxford: Pergamon Press.

Rachman, S. (1973). The effects of psychological treatment. In H. J. Eysenck (Ed.), (pp. 805–861). *Handbook of abnormal psychology.* New York: Basic Books.

Rachman, S. J., & Wilson, G. T. (1980). *The effects of psychological therapy* (2nd ed.). New York: Pergamon Press.

Reik, T. (1948). *Listening with the third ear.* New York: Farrar, Straus.

Report of the Research Task Force of the National Institute of Mental Health (1975). *Research in the Service of Mental Health.* DHEW Publication No. (ADM) 75–236. Rockville, MD.

Rivero, A. (1977). The therapy game. *St. Louisan 9,* p. 49.

Rogers, C. R. (1951). *Client-centered therapy.* Boston: Houghton Mifflin.

Rosenbaum, C. P. (1964). Events of early therapy and brief therapy. *Archives of General Psychiatry, 10,* 506–512.

Rosenzweig, S. (1936). Some implicit common factors in diverse methods of psychotherapy. *American Journal of Orthopsychiatry, 6,* 412–415.

Rush, A. J., Beck, A. T., Kovacs, M., & Hollon, S. (1977). Comparative efficacy of cognitive therapy and pharmacotherapy in the treatment of depressed outpatients. *Cognitive Therapy and Research, 1,* 17–37.

Sachs, J. S. (1983). Negative factors in brief psychotherapy: An empirical assessment. *Journal of Consulting and Clinical Psychology, 51,* 557–564.

Salter, A. (1949). *Conditioned reflex therapy.* New York: Farrar, Straus.

Schmideberg, M. (1958). Values and goals in psychotherapy. *The Psychiatric Quarterly, 32,* 233–265.

Schofield, W. (1988). *Pragmatics of psychotherapy. A survey of theories and practices.* New Brunswick, NJ: Transaction Books.

Shlien, J. M. (1957). Time-limited psychotherapy: An experimental investigation of practical values and theoretical implications. *Journal of Counseling Psychology, 4,* 318–323.

Shlien, J. M., Mosak, H. H., & Dreikurs, R. (1962). Effect of time limits: A comparison of two psychotherapies. *Journal of Counseling Psychology, 31–34.*

Sifneos, P. E. (1965). Seven-years experience with short-term dynamic psychotherapy. *Proceedings of the 6th International Congress of Psychotherapy,* Selected Lectures, (pp. 127–135). London 1964, Basel/New York: S. Karger.

Sifneos, P. E. (1981). Short-term anxiety provoking psychotherapy: Its history, technique, outcome, and instruction. In S. H. Budman (Ed.), (pp. 45–81). *Forms of brief therapy.* New York: Guilford Press.

Sloane, R. B., Staples, F. R., Cristol, A. H., Yorkston, N. J., & Whipple, K. (1975). *Psychotherapy versus behavior therapy.* Cambridge, MA: Harvard University Press.

Smith, D. (1982). Trends in counseling and psychotherapy. *American Psychologist, 37,*

802–809.

Smith, M. L., & Glass, G. V. (1977). Meta-analysis of psychotherapy outcome studies. *American Psychologist, 32*, 752–760.

Smith, M. L., Glass, G. V., & Miller, T. I. (1980). *The benefits of psychotherapy.* Baltimore: The Johns Hopkins University Press.

Stieper, D. R., & Wiener, D. N. (1959). The problem of interminability in outpatient psychotherapy. *Journal of Consulting Psychology, 23*, 237–242.

Stieper, D. R., & Weiner, D. N. (1965). *Dimensions of psychotherapy: An experimental and clinical approach.* Chicago: Aldine.

Strupp, H. H., & Binder, J. L. (1984). *Psychotherapy in a new key. A guide to time-limited dynamic psychotherapy.* New York: Basic Books.

Strupp, H. H., & Hadley, S. W. (1977). A tripartite model of mental health and therapeutic outcomes: With special reference to negative effects in psychotherapy. *American Psychologist, 32*, 187–196.

Swann, G. E., & MacDonald, M. L. (1978). Behavior therapy in practice: A national survey of behavior therapists. *Behavior Therapy, 9*, 799–807.

Swartz, J. (1969). Time-limited brief psychotherapy. *Seminars in Psychiatry, 1*, 380–388.

Thompson, L. W., Gallagher, D., & Breckenridge, J. S. (1987). Comparative effectiveness of psychotherapies for depressed elders. *Journal of Consulting and Clinical Psychology, 55*, 385–390.

Truax, C. B. (1966). Reinforcement and nonreinforcement in Rogerian psychotherapy. *Journal of Abnormal Psychology, 71*, 1–9.

van Kalmthout, M. A., Schaap, C., & Wojciechowski, F. L. (1985). *Common factors in psychotherapy.* Lisse, The Netherlands: Swets & Zeitlinger.

Wachtel, P. L. (1977). *Psychoanalysis and behavior therapy.* New York: Basic Books.

Weiss, L., Katzman, M., & Wolchik, S. (1985). *Treating bulimia. A psychoeducational approach.* New York: Pergamon Press.

Weissman, M. M., Prusoff, B. A., DiMascio, A., Neu, C., Gokloney, M., & Klerman, G. L. (1979). The efficacy of drugs and psychotherapy in the treatment of acute depressive episodes. *American Journal of Psychiatry, 136*, 555–558.

White, H. S., Burke, J. D., Jr., & Havens, L. L. (1981). Choosing a method of short-term therapy: A developmental approach. In S. H. Budman (Ed.), (pp. 243–267). *Forms of brief therapy.* New York: Guilford.

Wolberg, L. R. (Ed.). (1965). *Short-term psychotherapy.* New York: Grune & Stratton.

Wolpe, J. (1958). *Psychotherapy by reciprocal inhibition.* Stanford, CA: Stanford University Press.

Wolpe, J. (1961). The systematic desensitization treatment of neuroses. *Journal of Nervous and Mental Disease, 132*, 181–203.

Yatus, A. J. (1970). *Behavior therapy.* New York: Wiley.

Zeiss, A., Lewinsohn, P., & Munoz, R. (1979). Nonspecific improvement effects in depression using interpersonal skills training, pleasant activities schedules, or cognitive training. *Journal of Consulting and Clinical Psychology, 47*, 427–439.

Author Index

Subject Index

About the Author

Sol L. Garfield, Professor Emeritus of Psychology at Washington University, received his PhD from Northwestern University in 1942. During World War II, he served as a clinical psychologist in the US Army and then worked as a chief psychologist in three clinical settings of the Veterans Administration. He has also directed three university doctoral programs in clinical psychology as well as a division of medical psychology. A former editor of the *Journal of Consulting and Clinical Psychology*, he has authored *Clinical Psychology: The Study of Personality and Behavior, Psychotherapy: An Eclectic Approach*, and with Allen E. Bergin is the editor of *The Handbook of Psychotherapy and Behavior Change*. He is an American Board of Professional Psychology diplomate, a fellow of the American Psychological Association, a former president of the Division of Clinical Psychology, and a former president of the Society of Psychotherapy Research. He has received several awards from the American Psychological Association.

Psychology Practitioner Guidebooks

Editors
Arnold P. Goldstein, Syracuse University
Leonard Krasner, Stanford University & SUNY at Stony Brook
Sol L. Garfield, Washington University in St. Louis

Patricia Lacks—BEHAVIORAL TREATMENT FOR PERSISTENT INSOMNIA

Arnold P. Goldstein & Harold Keller—AGGRESSIVE BEHAVIOR: Assessment and Intervention

C. Eugene Walker, Barbara L. Bonner & Keith L. Kaufman—THE PHYSICALLY AND SEXUALLY ABUSED CHILD: Evaluation and Treatment

Robert E. Becker, Richard G. Heimberg & Alan S. Bellack—SOCIAL SKILLS TRAINING TREATMENT FOR DEPRESSION

Richard F. Dangel & Richard A. Polster—TEACHING CHILD MANAGEMENT SKILLS

Albert Ellis, John F. McInerney, Raymond DiGiuseppe & Raymond Yeager—RATIONAL-EMOTIVE THERAPY WITH ALCOHOLICS AND SUBSTANCE ABUSERS

Johnny L. Matson & Thomas H. Ollendick—ENHANCING CHILDREN'S SOCIAL SKILLS: Assessment and Training

Edward B. Blanchard, John E. Martin & Patricia M. Dubbert—NON-DRUG TREATMENTS FOR ESSENTIAL HYPERTENSION

Samuel M. Turner & Deborah C. Beidel—TREATING OBSESSIVE-COMPULSIVE DISORDER

Alice W. Pope, Susan M. McHale & W. Edward Craighead—SELF-ESTEEM ENHANCEMENT WITH CHILDREN AND ADOLESCENTS

Jean E. Rhodes & Leonard A. Jason—PREVENTING SUBSTANCE ABUSE AMONG CHILDREN AND ADOLESCENTS

Gerald D. Oster, Janice E. Caro, Daniel R. Eagen & Margaret A. Lillo—ASSESSING ADOLESCENTS

Robin C. Winkler, Dirck W. Brown, Margaret van Keppel & Amy Blanchard—CLINICAL PRACTICE IN ADOPTION

Roger Poppen—BEHAVIORAL RELAXATION TRAINING AND ASSESSMENT

Michael D. LeBow—ADULT OBESITY THERAPY

Robert Paul Liberman, William J. De Risi & Kim T. Mueser—SOCIAL SKILLS TRAINING FOR PSYCHIATRIC PATIENTS

Johnny L. Matson—TREATING DEPRESSION IN CHILDREN AND ADOLESCENTS